CW00850698

# THE PILOT AND
# THE COMMANDO

# THE PILOT AND THE COMMANDO

*The interlinked lives of two young Christians in the Second World War*

ANTHONY MEREDITH

authorHOUSE®

AuthorHouse™
1663 Liberty Drive
Bloomington, IN 47403
www.authorhouse.com
Phone: 1-800-839-8640

© 2011 by Anthony Meredith. All rights reserved.

No part of this book may be reproduced, stored in a retrieval system, or transmitted by any means without the written permission of the author.

First published by AuthorHouse    12/17/2011

ISBN: 978-1-4678-7761-9 (sc)
ISBN: 978-1-4678-7762-6 (ebk)

Printed in the United States of America

Any people depicted in stock imagery provided by Thinkstock are models, and such images are being used for illustrative purposes only.
Certain stock imagery © Thinkstock.

This book is printed on acid-free paper.

Because of the dynamic nature of the Internet, any web addresses or links contained in this book may have changed since publication and may no longer be valid. The views expressed in this work are solely those of the author and do not necessarily reflect the views of the publisher, and the publisher hereby disclaims any responsibility for them.

# CONTENTS

# PREFACE

That *The Pilot And The Commando* describes the wartime exploits of my wife's father and uncle has made its research and writing a particular pleasure. Such a close family connection, of course, could easily mean a loss of biographical objectivity, but there are a number of encouraging precedents. Nearly two thousand years ago, for example, the great Roman historian Tacitus produced a memoir of *his* father-in-law, Agricola, a splendidly incisive text enjoyed by generations of Latin students. Our pilot and commando may not have reached the same exalted heights as Gnaeus Julius Agricola (who, while squashing the unruly Britons, became the island's governor-general), yet their experiences also touch on major events and have a very great deal to say about the pity of war.

I knew Jos Nicholl, the commando, well, for he and I were also colleagues for several years at the same school, but I never met David Carter, the pilot. Yet I came to know him well, too, for when, some time after his death, I started reading through an archive of David's letters, diaries and notebooks, chronicling a very busy life (five years of which were spent as a pilot with the Fleet Air Arm), I was struck not only by the compelling nature of the subject matter but also the immense security of his Christian faith, finding it so challenging and moving, indeed, that I attempted to put his story into a coherent narrative form. A draft was eventually cyclostyled and circulated around family and friends, but the further revision it needed somehow never quite happened.

That was nearly thirty years (and a dozen books) ago. Then, one day rather more recently, in trying to clear up some overburdened cupboards, I came across another piece of writing which had similarly been duplicated and sent round to family and friends: *The Cross Still Stands*, Jos Nicholl's wartime story, written with the clear intention of honouring the fellow commandos who had perished when fighting alongside him. His descriptions of the war were as vivid as David's. The two experiences, indeed, were clearly complementary, and the idea arose of a joint narrative showing a naval airman and an army commando whose fortitude and faith were tested to the very limits. There was a gloriously happy ending, too, for the pilot married the commando's sister in the very first days of peace.

There was just one snag. Whereas David's inner thoughts were well documented, Jos's seemed not to be, for *The Cross Still Stands* is essentially military history, modestly excluding self. Then a whole cache of long-lost letters were found, written by Jos to his parents and other close family members during the war. At one stroke, the impasse had vanished, and in due course the interlinked story of the two very different wartime experiences emerged. There is much heroism within both narratives, though David and Jos would have disclaimed any suggestion of being heroic. They would have simply seen themselves as two ordinary, peace-loving young men who, like many hundreds of thousands of others, happened to be faced with extraordinary circumstances and the direst of situations.

But why write about them now, when the Second World War is as much a piece of ancient history as Tacitus's *Agricola*? Why add a small postscript to the war's vast literature? Don't we have enough current wars of our own without worrying about those in the past? And why write of faith in a secular age? Do this old-time pilot and commando have any possible relevance to our modern world of broken economies, communities, celebrities and families? I believe they do.

I am hugely grateful to the encouragement and help received from all the various strands of the Carter and Nicholl families, not least from David and Jos' children, Heather, Rachel, Robert, Angela, Anthony, Richard and Jonathan. There has been great support too from many members of Stowe Church.

Tony Meredith
Akeley
November 2011

# 1
# THE PRELUDE TO WAR

In 1939 two Christian friends in the same Cambridge college, David Carter and Jos Nicholl, found their university careers brought to a sudden end by the outbreak of war with Nazi Germany. In due course David became a Fleet Air Arm pilot and Jos an Army Commando. Their subsequent wartime experiences offer some vivid insights into what it meant to be a young person caught up in the horrors of the Second World War and the extent to which a Christian faith might endure and inspire in such challenging times. This war, of course, has now become the stuff of history books, and, though the ever-inventive entertainment industry has ensured that Hitler's Third Reich remains in the public consciousness, post-war social developments have radically altered the world in which David and Jos grew up.

England in the Twenties and Thirties was a much more insular country than it is today, with some 20 million less inhabitants and a distinctly narrower cultural background. Superficially, the recently concluded war-to-end-all-wars had changed very little. The same closely-knit upper-class establishment still paced the corridors of power; Britannia still ruled the waves; and maps in school atlases still marked large chunks of the world in red to signify participation in the mighty British Empire. Social change was, of course, afoot. In David's Surrey and Jos's Sussex, for example, the proliferation of rows of smart suburban terraces were tokens of a new emerging middle-class, whilst for those in the older, more prosperous professions there were often ampler homes, usually with a few acres of grounds, a resident maid or two and a couple of vintage motor cars, ready to roam the country's charmingly rustic and deserted roads. Both boys were lucky that their families were part of this more affluent group. David Carter, who was two years old at the end of the First World War, was the son of a stockbroker who worked in the family's long-established firm in the City and was a pillar of his local church and whist club. Jos Nicholl, born in 1920, had a father who was similarly respected, a doctor with a flourishing practice in Lewes.

History books tend to depict the Twenties as extremely turbulent and even 'Roaring', but the Carters and Nicholls were unaffected by the more extrovert excitements cheering up the post-war gloom. Their world had no meeting-point with jazz or the 'Bright Young Things' who championed lively new dance-tunes like the Charleston. Nor were they particularly moved by the proliferating mass entertainments such as professional football and the raucous Talkies, or the cults of speed and celebrity enthusiastically promoted by the fast-developing media - all those airships, monster racing cars, record-breaking ocean liners and dare-devil solo pilots. Both families would have had more time for *Winnie-the-Pooh* than that other new arrival of the 1920s, *The Great Gatsby*, for the Carters and Nicholls were essentially conservative and gentle people, looking back to the secure Edwardian days with a certain nostalgia.

High Beech, where David Carter was born and brought up, fitted this mood exactly: an imposing Edwardian red-brick house, specially built for his father near the Surrey village of South Nutfield. On a clear day High Beech enjoyed stunning views across open countryside to Chanctonbury Ring and the spires of East Grinstead. The young Jos Nicholl was similarly fortunate. After spells in Lewes and abroad, he lived at Ades, another imposing red-brick house, though dating further back, to the 1820s, in the village of Chailey, a few miles outside Lewes.

Both boys came from families of ample Edwardian dimensions, David being the third of six children, and Jos the second of five. Both also had families with long traditions of Christian philanthropy and service, another trait which perhaps was more characteristic of the era before the First World War. The Carters, who were related to the prison reformer Elizabeth Fry, had been involved in the founding of several schools and mission halls as well as the early endeavours of Dr Barnardo and the temperance movement. David's father led regular prayers for the family and servants each day at High Beech, and at work high-mindedly refused to have anything to do with brewery and armament shares. Sunday at High Beech was still very much the Lord's day, with no newspapers allowed and the children's reading vetted to ensure its propriety.

David's parents, Robert and Rachel Carter

The Nicholls were as equally committed as the Carters to good causes. Jos's mother was the daughter of missionaries, and when Jos was only two his father began five years as a surgeon at the Church Mission Society's hospital at Quetta, a large but undeveloped town close to the modern Pakistan-Afghanistan border. It was a brave move to take the family to the Indian subcontinent. Jos at the time was one of three small children, and a fourth, Joanna, was born while they were there. At Quetta Jos's parents and grandmother committed themselves devotedly to their missionary work, so he spent a great deal of time with a nanny. He and his brother Geoffrey taught themselves to read, sitting on their bungalow verandah, observed as often as not by some less than friendly vultures in a nearby tree. Rather more comforting were the goats each child kept as a pet.

A boarding school education followed as a matter of course. By the age of eight David was happily settled at Sutherland House in Windlesham, Surrey, known today as Woodcote House but then a small establishment run by a Christian couple called Bradnack whose Dickensian name belied their kindly nature.

Jos (right) with his parents, his brothers and sister Joanna, 1927

Over the next six years David happily assimilated Sutherland House's strong Christian atmosphere and embraced with enthusiasm the importance assigned to the games field, which, fortunately, was where he most excelled. Many a small silver cup, the spoils of a sports day, still survives, beautifully engraved. So, too, a prized John Wisden cricket ball with a silver plaque telling of wickets taken with four consecutive deliveries in a school match in the golden summer of 1930.

The Nicholls on their return from India sent Jos to Great Walstead, a prep school which had recently taken over a rambling house in many country acres outside Hayward's Heath. 'Pop' Nicholl also agreed to add the role of school doctor to his busy practice. With its relaxed ethos of 'mud and love', Great Walstead was most unusual in its day, almost to the point of eccentricity. The headmaster's chief preoccupation was said to be his Sunday sermons, for which he would spend much time on making impressive models to use as visual aids. His teaching in the rest of the week seems to have been less passionate, Jos's brother Geoffrey later recalling that "we made scant academic progress with him, learning no Latin at all, though he and I once raced each other in making wirelesses."

David dressed up for the camera, c.1923

Jos (right) with Pat, Geoffrey and Joanna

It was through Great Walstead, in the late 1920s, that the Carter and Nicholl families first came to know each other. David's father, impressed by what he had heard about it, sent Andrew, his youngest son, there, and Andrew quickly made friends with Jos's younger brother, Pat. A deep friendship between both sets of parents and children rapidly developed from the moment they participated in the same holiday in Devon run by the Children's Special Service Mission. Further shared holidays of a similar nature followed.

David excelled in athletics and swimming even more than cricket, and when he moved on to St Lawrence College, Ramsgate, he was equally outstanding in rugby and hockey. In due course he became a deputy head boy notable for mature leadership qualities, his quiet profession of faith being balanced by a huge sense of fun and zest for living. "It was not just that he earned the respect of his peers," recalled his brother Stephen, "so much as his unusual ability to get the best out of every single person." Stephen often accompanied David on holiday expeditions by bicycle - they were later to share an elderly motorbike - to favourite places like Brooklands, the Reigate squash courts and Croydon Airport ("where, if we were lucky, there would be the excitement of a plane landing every half hour").

In 1936 David won a place at Cambridge to read Mathematics. By this time Jos was starting his third year at Stowe School near Buckingham. Jos and his brothers were lucky in their housemaster there, a vivid character, the towering Revd Humphrey Playford, a former pilot in the First World War, Cambridge rowing blue and winner of the Henley Diamond Sculls, who drove an open Bentley around the country roads with great zest. A larger-than-life figure of strong opinions, known to be quite combative in the Common Room, Playford probably helped broaden Jos's thinking, which had been largely influenced by Crusader camps and those run at Eastbourne (the forerunner of Iwerne) by that most powerful of evangelical clergymen, E. J. H. Nash, affectionately known as 'Bash'.

Hitler had seized power in Germany only the year before Jos reached Stowe, and the possibility of another world war was soon to become a dominant issue. Jos's first term had been memorable for a passionate sermon given on Remembrance Sunday by the headmaster, J.F. Roxburgh:

War is the supreme folly of civilisation and cannot begin without hatred, nor continue without lies ... Let us resolve then, as far as we can affect the issue, that our country shall work throughout the world for justice, truth and the rule of law ...

Alas, peace with honour proved a lost cause. After the Munich crisis Jos joined the rest of the school digging trenches in case of sudden invasion. Each evening there would be groups of boys huddled around in studies and in houserooms listening to the latest news as (in the words of the school magazine) "the hoarse shouts of a united Germany came over the wireless". It was against such a tense background that Jos enjoyed his sixth-form years, becoming a dashing wing-three quarter in the 1st XV, a prefect and Head of House. Although the hoarse shouts had grown hoarser, war had still not arrived when, in the spring of 1939, he left Stowe and spent the summer teaching at a prep school. War was finally declared on 3 September, just as he was preparing to join David at Queens' College, Cambridge, where he was to read History.

Jos (back row, left) with his parents plus Pat, Geoffrey, Joanna
and (with the dogs) Charitie, 1939

Queens' College, founded in the fifteenth century and charmingly
situated either side of the river Cam, was by this time something of a
Carter-Nicholl enclave. David's elder brother, Roderick Carter, had already
been through Queens' and was now training for the church; his younger
brother, Stephen, was in his second year, studying Natural Sciences; so too
Jos's eldest brother, Geoffrey Nicholl; David himself would have left by now
but for his constant struggle with Maths which had resulted in a fourth-year
diversion to Economics and General Science.

Jos loved Cambridge from the moment he first arrived. He later
recalled:

I was lucky to be able to have rooms in College in my first year - usually the
first year was spent out. Geoff and Stephen were sharing a large room in the
Kent Building (K2) and in the Lent Term I joined them. It was a wonderful
year. David was fly-half and captain of the Queens' XV, Geoff was full-back
and I was on the wing. A great friend of ours, Maurice Wood, later the
Bishop of Norwich, was a wing-forward. Although we had no Blues in
the team we got through to the Final of Cuppers, only to find ourselves

up against St John's who had 5 Blues. In the end we lost, but it was a great game! And there was a great dinner afterwards!

Jos was delighted that David was a member of that exclusive social club of Cambridge sportsmen, Hawks - "So he was able to recommend first Geoff and Stephen and then me!" And when David and Stephen organised a London–Brighton relay-walk between Cambridge and Oxford, the Nicholls were of course there supporting the Carters.

The newly declared war hung heavily over all this jollity, putting it into sharp relief. Before coming up Jos had visited a Naval Recruiting Office, but was turned down because of poor eyesight, so early on in his first term he applied to join the Army, was summoned to the Cambridge Senate House and duly handed the King's shilling. He also enlisted in the University Senior Training Corps. David, meanwhile, having some time earlier joined the Royal Naval Volunteer Reserve, hoped to qualify as a pilot with the Fleet Air Arm. He had always nursed a passion for flying, and, unlike Jos, who was never one of the world's natural drivers or mechanics, had a flair for all things mechanical. David had anticipated spending a full final year at Cambridge, but the swift introduction of War Emergency Exams allowed him to take his degree that December.

Jos retained vivid memories of David in the one term they shared together at Cambridge:

They were, despite everything, happy, careless days, with highlights like evening skating trips and jolly meetings of the Kangaroo Club, the college's own dining club for the sportier types. David was always the wise, elder statesman, who could act as a steadying influence on Fresher enthusiasm! Somehow we couldn't think of him except as 'Dear David'. Looking back, I can see it was something of the saintliness of his character which impressed everyone so much about him. Then there were his splendidly written letters which ended with the catch phrase of the moment. 'Pip Pip for the present' was the usual one. Others included 'Yours to a cinder'.

Jos marvelled at David's unconcerned attitude to public transport:

He used to say things like, 'Oh, I catch trains as they come'. It wasn't happy-go-lucky. It was an other-worldliness and detachment (which of course could be unintentionally aggravating to family and friends on occasion). But it inspired a depth of friendship and understanding which was very, very special. It was an absolute privilege, at Cambridge and ever afterwards, to be his friend.

Both David and Jos participated as a matter of course in the Cambridge Inter-Collegiate Christian Union. On Sunday mornings there were large gatherings at the Henry Martyn Hall for Bible readings; crowded winter evening services took place at the nearby Holy Trinity Church; and, in the summer, there was an hour's informal service in the Market Square, when fifty or so would gather round a piano or harmonium, lifted onto a platform or even the back of a lorry, attracting friends and passers-by till two or three hundred would be gathered around. Equally prominent in Cambridge at this time was Frank Buchman's Oxford Group (later known as Moral Re-Armament), which had been acquiring world-wide influence. The Group, with its insistence on the Four Absolutes - absolute honesty, purity, unselfishness and love - had, as Jos later noted, "deepened David's faith and strengthened his devotional life". Frank Buchman's initiative for the spread of world peace and universal love had matched the mood of the late 1930s, and Buchman had even attempted to convert Germany's leaders, having no less than three interviews with Heinrich Himmler (which led to fierce accusations that he was soft on Hitler). But in 1939 the idealistic David saw only potential good coming from Buchman's Group, and all his life he was to draw much inspiration from the Four Absolutes.

Having obtained his rushed degree that Christmas and having been accepted for the Fleet Air Arm, David readied himself for active service in 1940. Jos, too, though temporarily staying on at Cambridge, realised his own call-up might quickly follow. Hitler's invasion of Poland had, at one stroke, meant the invasion and imminent break-up of their own secure and privileged world.

# 2

# DAVID: TRAINING ON A SWORDFISH

The Navy seemed in no rush for David's services. On discovering that he would not be called up for two or three months, he followed Jos's example and worked temporarily at a prep school, Ardvreck, in the very heart of Scotland, on the edge of Crieff and the wild Perthshire hills. The spring term of 1940 was marked by long periods of snow and freezing temperatures, but David enjoyed it all, enthusiastically leading the skating when the burn at the bottom of the cricket field froze. Twice at short notice he took the place of a visiting Bishop and gave an address to the school on a Sunday night. Most evenings he would stay up late with a few other teachers discussing the current 'Phoney War'. (The British Expeditionary Force was still in France, seemingly secure behind the Maginot Line which guarded the border with Germany.) In his one brief term at Ardvreck David made a lasting impression. "I remember him," wrote one of his colleagues thirty years afterwards, "as a quiet and modest person, with a delightful sense of fun, and one whose whole life radiated a profound Christian faith . . ."

David's call-up coincided with the end of the 'Phoney War' in May 1940, when the Nazis invaded France via the low countries, the British retreated to the Channel, Winston Churchill took over as Prime Minister, and the evacuation from Dunkirk enabled defeat to be softened by stories of heroism. As the war gathered momentum during the rest of that year, David completed his basic training, qualified for a commission and, as Sub-Lieutenant Carter, gained his wings at the Netheravon training school. Its airfield, on a bleak part of Salisbury Plain, was a challenging place, its shapeless landing strip containing several hazards: the ground sometimes rose or fell away by fifty feet; flocks of sheep, too, sometimes grazed unconcernedly across the landing strip. From Wiltshire he went for further training to Scotland, to Crail on the East Fife coast, where the aerodrome was even bleaker, a scene of utter desolation. The runways had just been completed. There was mud everywhere. It was bitingly cold. David was kept very busy, however, in a strenuous programme using tired versions of the veteran biplane, the Fairey Swordfish. He was taught how to drop torpedoes, to fly in formation and to fly at night, and, most important of all, the technique of landing on an aircraft carrier. Taking off proved a comparatively simple operation, a question of opening up the throttle and keeping the aircraft straight till airborne. But with some carrier decks being not much wider than twenty yards, there was little room for error in landing, especially when the carrier could be steaming away at 10-20 knots, its deck pitching in the swell.

However good a pilot might be, he depended ultimately on the judgement of the batsman, who stood on the port side of the vessel, near the end of the deck. The batsman held a yellow circular disc in each hand, with which he gave signals to the pilot - higher! faster! slower! - which were to be obeyed without fail. If the approach went wrong, the batsman circled a bat around his head, indicating the need to abort and try again. If the approach went according to plan, the batsman would signal the pilot to cut his engine, when a few feet off the deck. With his engine cut, the pilot then depended on being stopped by a system of arrestor wires, which were raised some six inches off the deck as the aircraft approached. The pilot lowered a hook and aimed to catch an arrestor wire with it. This done, a Swordfish would be stationary in thirty yards. If the pilot did not manage to catch the wire, then he would be stopped, abruptly and painfully, by a safety cable and wire barrier, without which he would crash into other aircraft parked further down the deck. It was a hazardous business.

After Crail's insights into the intricacies of carrier life, David was sent on a gunnery course at Worthy Down near Winchester, a Fleet Air Arm station with a dangerously undulating grass strip as a runway and the actor Ralph Richardson as its current commander. Such were the perils of Worthy Down that just a few months later another young pilot, Laurence Olivier, not only wrecked one aircraft but damaged another two when merely taxi-ing down the runway before take-off. David proved rather more successful, and soon learnt how to operate the Swordfish's fixed, forward-firing Vickers machine-gun, but, as some cynics were not slow to observe, a Swordfish pilot did not really need such a course, as every enemy warplane would be at least twice as fast as his, and he would be more gunned at than gunning.

David's final period of training was spent at the Royal Naval College, Greenwich. It was now early 1941, the time of the London blitz. Every night for several months David's parents watched the skies turn red from their temporary home in Reigate (the Army having requisitioned High Beech). One entry in David's diary vividly recalls a difficult return from Reigate to Greenwich (in 'Archie', an old, bull-nosed Morris which he had recently inherited from elder brother Roderick) and the horrors of the blitz:

A tricky drive in a heavy air raid. Very definitely frightened! A fierce glow all along the river. I cautiously approached from the south making a wide detour. There have been heavy air-raids this month. The second Fire of London. Heavy frosts too. Archie frozen solid for days. Heavy talks by Commander Street. I remember standing on the river bank in front of Greenwich one morning after one of the worst raids. The opposite bank presented an uninterrupted scene of desolation as far as the eye can reach. A canopy of black smoke drifts slowly across. It is coming from the heart of the city and obscures the entire sky. It is very dark now, but the river traffic carries stubbornly, almost blindly, on . . .

# 3

## JOS WITH THE ROYAL ARTILLERY

Jos had still been studying at Cambridge while David was at Ardvreck, and around the time the Germans invaded the low countries he had taken his first-year exams. The dramatically swift fall of France, however, brought an abrupt end to his life as an undergraduate:

I had been playing tennis, mixed doubles. Afterwards, the four of us cycled back to the Old Court. I can remember feeling very content. Exams were over and May Week lay ahead. The girls were listening politely as I explained the workings of the College's famous renaissance sundial, when a voice echoed over the quad: 'Have you heard? The college has got to be evacuated tomorrow.' We rushed to the notice - board in the Porter's Lodge. Yes, it was true. Undergraduates had to pack and leave the next day. The College was to become a hospital to house the casualties expected from France . . .

Back at his Sussex home, Jos waited for his call-up, working meanwhile on a nearby farm and serving with the Local Defence Volunteers (later to be named the Home Guard).

For a spirited 20 - year - old who approached life much as he did his rugby football - with the passion of a hard - charging wing three - quarter - the summer of 1940 proved a frustration as he followed the course of the Battle of Britain on the radio and sometimes, also, in the skies above him. Many of his contemporaries were already in the Forces. Even his old housemaster at Stowe, the Reverend Humphrey Playford, now rising 40, had managed to be driving ambulances in Nazi - threatened France (before beating a hasty retreat). So it was a relief when, that September, Jos finally received his papers, passed his medical A1 and began his training as Gunner

J. Nicholl (of J Squad, H Battalion), reporting to the Royal Artillery's Heavy Anti-Aircraft Training Unit at Blackdown, near Haslemere.

Initially his letters home were full of enthusiasm for the new life, particularly when he was moved from Haslemere to a Cornish training camp, 7 miles up the coast from Bude, and found himself with a unit operating two huge anti - aircraft guns, each gun requiring about 20 men. It was an exciting moment when they fired their first rounds:

On Friday our section fired at the sleeve towed by an aero. We got off about 10 rounds on the two guns and some said there was some pretty good shooting . . . The sleeve went into a cloud after we had fired and when it came out again it was tattered! The bang was pretty startling, but I hope we'll get over this soon.

In November 1940, he took the first steps towards becoming an officer. After passing a difficult interview before the O.C.T.U. board at Aldershot – "They told me I had passed but to uphold their recommendation I should be more tidy!" – he spent four months as an officer cadet at Shrivenham, deep in the Wiltshire countryside not far from Swindon. It was a big base, turning out over 100 new officers each month. There was much tedious army routine – notably the repetitive learning of how to salute and do drill – but worst of all were the manuals of theoretical physics and the constant scientific lectures. The study of magnetism and the composition of carbon held little interest for him and this probably showed, for he was soon relegated from guns to searchlights.

The disappointment he felt at this relegation was not even offset by the excitement of two serious games of rugby a week and having the England cricketer Stan Nichols as his P.E. instructor and the Kent leg-spinner Doug Wright as a fellow cadet. His fate seemed all the worse when he had recently come across a Conscientious Objector friend who had been having an exciting time re-laying railway sleepers, bombed at Swindon, in the actual course of German air attacks. A tentative transfer request was speedily turned down by the Royal Artillery. A more positive attitude, he was informed, was expected of an officer cadet.

Shrivenham was also a disappointment in its attitude to religion. "It seems so impossible here to believe that this is a Christian country," he wrote despondently to his brother Pat. And a little later, to his parents: "The problem is to find anyone else among the 1,600 officer cadets who is also interested in reading the Bible." He was particularly dejected by the compulsory Church Parades and the apathetic reaction towards them.

Occasionally, however, he was able to utilise short leaves to visit friends, particularly those from Cambridge:

Had a grand time with Maurice Wood. He told me Mark Ruston was now at Woking and very lonely . . . I got there at 5.00 and managed to hunt him out. He was having a confirmation class in his rooms, so I stayed and listened. (It was rather different from one of Humphrey's at school!) And then he made me stay for supper. Altogether it was a grand day.

As exams proliferated and his emergence as a fully-fledged officer grew nearer, he renewed his efforts to move out of the Royal Artillery into something of greater appeal to his fighting spirit, only to be told firmly that officers working on the crucial air defences of Great Britain were under no circumstances to be redeployed. When, in March 1941, he was finally commissioned, he was sent to a Derbyshire village, better known for its Morris dancing than its antipathy to the Third Reich. The London Blitz was still at its height, but his new Battery unit, held in reserve, illuminated only empty skies.

In May 1941 there was a brief flutter of hope when he was transferred to Warwickshire, but though there was a mass bomber attack on Birmingham that month, his Battery continued to stay in reserve. He felt distinctly guilty that in his off-duty hours he was able to cycle in to Stratford to see *The Taming of the Shrew* and Aston Cantlow to visit Mary Arden's house. He celebrated his 21st birthday with a punting trip on the Avon. He also pedalled off to several local churches, his dismay at his current posting possibly contributing to some naively censorious views. ("As usual in this vicinity," he told his parents on one occasion, "the church had a full quota of altars and candles.")

Jos as a newly commissioned Royal Artillery officer

The war, meanwhile, was entering a new phase. The Blitz had come to an end, lessening Jos's immediate chances of lighting up the Luftwaffe for the gunners. Sent on a course to observe the operations room at Baginton Aerodrome near the heavily blitzed city of Coventry, he saw first-hand the realities of war and the kind of situation other, less lucky anti-aircraft batteries must have been facing during the Battle of Britain's worst trials:

Smoke generators lay grim and frightening on the grass verge beside the main road. They were lit each night to send a nauseating smell and a depressing gloom over the already sombre city. In the main shopping centre not only were there still gaping holes in the roads indifferently cordoned off, the crazily balanced outer walls of houses and shops, and the universal smell of smouldering wood and rubber, but, worst of all, the odour of shattered sewers. No unboiled water could be drunk, and the chlorine in what could be used made a cup of tea an agony. Over the grim silence of the dead city there stood the husk of a shattered Cathedral.

While he was at Baginton, he was interested to hear talk in the officers' mess of a "first-rate crowd of commandos based at Largs in Scotland", where a Major Jack Churchill was said to be the key personality. So Jos wrote to him, and a reply came back suggesting that the newly-formed Special Services Brigade might well be interested in him, if he could get a transfer. So he tried again, but still couldn't. In despair, he wrote again to Largs, expressing his frustrations. There were no current vacancies in No. 3 Commando, came Churchill's response, but why didn't he put his name on their waiting list? He did so, but with a sinking heart, convinced it would not lead to anything. Feeling in helpless thrall to the Artillery, he resolutely braced himself for further fatuous manoeuvres in the heart of sleepy Warwickshire.

# 4

# DAVID WITH THE ARK ROYAL

David's months of intense training concluded excitingly with the news, in March 1941, of a posting to the Fleet Air Arm's 816 Squadron which was regrouping after suffering big losses and now joining the aircraft-carrier *HMS Ark Royal* in the Mediterranean. Launched in 1937, the third of five ships to bear the name, the *Ark* had already been much in the news and only a month earlier a strike force of 15 of her Swordfish had played a leading role in sinking the German battleship *Bismarck*. With her enormous hangars which ran the length of the ship and accommodated 60 aircraft, her three lifts which conveyed the machines to and from the landing deck, her two catapults for take-offs, and her crash barrier and arrestor wires working on the very latest hydraulic principles, the *Ark Royal* boasted some of the most up-to-date aircraft-carrier technology.

David sailed out with his new colleagues to the Mediterranean in another, older carrier, *HMS Furious*, which was ferrying some RAF Hurricanes to the beleaguered island of Malta. *Furious* had an illustrious history which extended back to 1918 and the British Navy's very first deck landing. A few senior members of 816 Squadron knew the *Furious* well, for they had been based on her when their Swordfish made the first aerial torpedo raid of the war, off Norway, as well as a brave attack on the giant battle-cruiser *Scharnhorst*.

The voyage out was marred by an accident to one of the Hurricanes, as it took off from the carrier to make the final part of the journey to Malta. Swerving across the deck, it hit the bridge, burst into flames and started a serious fire. Fourteen men were killed. At 24 David was face to face with the realities of active service for the first time. The effect was to strengthen his realisation of the need to speak about his faith more openly, something which seemed far from easy in the rough and tumble of wartime life. Towards the end of his journey on *Furious*, David wrote to his parents:

You mustn't think that what follows is in any way morbid. How can it be, when death for Christians is to be with Him? Neither am I saying it because I feel myself in any particular danger. But I do feel that the times are such that we should be prepared and *willing* that each letter could be the last. That being so, I feel this is too important to be left unsaid: I feel exceedingly guilty about the way I have failed to speak to others about my Saviour . . . It is only when you come across sudden death in the way we have that you realise how completely *empty* is life without Christ. And it's only then, too, that one sees how utterly despicable and selfish is one's own diffidence and shyness.

But even in my failure I have been conscious of God's very nearness and understanding. Here is just one example. Mr Sidlow Baxter gave me a book of his, *The Best Word Ever*, when I was in Edinburgh last. On board ship I lost it amongst other things (at that time I was sleeping and had all my possessions in a kind of public gangway). Two days later, a young fellow, whom, though not a pilot, I had been seeing quite a lot, was killed. I was feeling very bad about this and the opportunity I had missed, when that evening his servant brought me the book and told me he'd found it under his pillow. There was a marker three-quarters of the way through . . .

816 Squadron eventually transferred from *Furious* to *Ark Royal*, operating from Gibraltar, and a quick familiarisation programme commenced. David, more used to flying from solid and dependable airfields than an unpredictable and lively ocean, found he had much to learn and not all his early deck landings went well. Indeed, on one occasion he came close to disaster, his Swordfish ending up badly damaged against the crash barrier.

The *Ark*, currently involved in a series of convoy runs, was a big and obvious target for enemy fire, and had already experienced several lucky escapes. In July David and his Swordfish were a tiny component in a massive operation to ferry over 5,000 men and 50,000 tons of stores to Malta in the face of unremitting attack from Italian E-boats and air attacks from Sardinia and Sicily. In this operation two other squadrons from the *Ark*'s company lost half their crews, but 816 survived intact.

The *Ark*'s next mission, a diversionary attack on the harbour town of Alghero, Majorca, revealed that there were other dangers for the pilots apart from those of enemy action. 9 Swordfish had bombed Alghero's aerodrome and all returned, but unfortunately one of them was still carrying a big bomb, which had 'hung up' in the racks. As this aircraft touched down, there was an enormous explosion, killing the pilot, his observer and air gunner as well as two officers and ratings of the *Ark*'s flight deck party. 6 of the Swordfish which had yet to land – one of them David's – were forced to circle the stricken ship for a considerable time as temporary repairs were made to the damaged deck and arrestor gear. His fuel gauge had been registering zero for quite a while before, to his huge relief, he was at last able to make his landing.

Nothing of the horrors of war came through in the letters David wrote to his parents. Deliberately, to allay fears, he avoided all mention of such dramas. Indeed, most of his letters contained very little about his flying. Of the voyage back from Alghero, for example, the most worrying thing he mentioned was the discomfort from the choppy seas. ("I don't think I find the motion *entirely* agreeable yet . . .")

The *Ark*'s next mission was an attack on Sardinia to attract as much enemy attention as possible while minefields were being laid off the Italian coast. The Swordfish crews had a dual role. Some attacked the city of Tempio and others, including David, were involved in a sweeping reconnaissance, trying to find the main Italian fleet, which, fortunately for them, was just a few miles outside their maximum range.

As August 1941 gave way to September, and the overwhelming Mediterranean heat cooled down a little, another big convoy was organised, Operation Halberd. A tough passage was assured.

David serving with *Ark Royal*, 1942

I'm starting this letter in the hope that I'll be able to get it off quickly when we touch land again. The next three days will be pretty tense, and I don't suppose I'll get much written then. If much does happen – we're ready for anything – you'll probably have heard about it before this reaches you! Anyway, just now it's rather like waiting for a rugger match, with a grim side thrown in, but although everyone is conscious of this, it does not weigh on our minds in the least. But what an advantage the Christian has!

The Italian fleet had closed in on the British, only to discover to its surprise that the allied convoy's strength was now greater than its own. As the Italians attempted to withdraw, David piloted one of the twelve Swordfish sent to try to slow down the Italians with torpedoes, but late or erroneous information prevented them making contact. After a vain search of many hours they returned wearily and landed in the dark in the middle of an attack by enemy E-boats, a perilous conclusion to a desperate day. "Four of us had less than 10 gallons of petrol between us," David noted. All the aircraft got down, though two were badly damaged in the process.

The dropping of torpedoes was a far from simple or safe operation for the Swordfish pilot, who had to fly very slowly and very low, about fifty feet above the sea. While he was concentrating on keeping his plane straight and level, during the dropping, he could do nothing about the tracer bullets flying towards him from heavily-defended ships. Had David's 12 Swordfish made contact with the Italian fleet, it is unlikely many of them would have returned.

The *Ark* was constantly out at sea, for between the big operations there was regular training. She had now done 200,000 miles without a proper refit and, because of this, Christmas at home was thought a strong possibility. "It will be funny to fly over land again!" David told his parents. "But then it will also be funny to see English women, children of any kind, and milk!" Meanwhile he and the other 1,600 members of the *Ark Royal* continued to keep alert:

I have told you before how busy I am? As a matter of fact, this squadron is improving daily in every respect. (I don't mean to say it's improving because I'm busy, but rather that I'm busy because it's improving!) We've got the grandest crowd of men for our ground-staff. My particular job enables me to take on occasions 'trouble' on their behalf. They are tremendously appreciative. I wonder if they realise how often I am disgustingly pleased with myself for taking 'trouble'? Too often I find myself amongst those of whom our Lord said 'they have their rewards'. I read somewhere that real kindness is to do 'the kindest possible thing in the kindest possible way'. I fall down on that. It usually requires too much self-effacement for me. I have a long way to go.

Great camaraderie existed not only with the ground crew but with the air crew too:

My observer continues to be a great delight to me. He is known in the squadron as 'the pocket observer'. He is very short. I cannot see round behind me, but they tell me he can just see over the cockpit edge, if he stands on the seat! He is only 21, and knows his stuff extremely well. Like me, at present he panics very easily. Happily, I find that if someone else panics, it has the best possible effect on me, so this suits me very well! His nervousness does not, I think, impair our safety at all, but only his peace of mind. Anyway, we are both improving, I think. He is not in the least afraid of outside dangers, but merely of making mistakes himself . . .

I don't think I described my air gunner? He's one of the youngest, very young for his age. And innocence personified! You know – 'Well, sir, I only . . .' Quite a good lad, I think, but my observer says he's lazy, and I'm having a special mirror fitted to see just what *does* go on behind!

David even had a few kind words for his Swordfish:

Unfortunately, my aeroplane won't go quite fast enough, but I don't want to change it, as it is fitted up with all my 'home comforts'. Anyway, you get rather attached to your machine when you've landed it safely a number of times.

Perhaps again to lessen the impression of danger in his parents' minds, he added:

While on the subject, I do also want to impress on you the safety of flying. You must all become air-minded because after the war you'll be behind the times if you aren't prepared to fly. So you might as well make up your minds now!

In November 1941, five months after David had joined her, *Ark Royal* took part in Operation Perpetual, which involved her in bringing more Hurricanes to Malta. This objective successfully accomplished, the carrier was on her way home to Gibraltar. There had been a brief flurry of anxiety when two sightings of German U-boats had been reported, but six Swordfish had flown off to look for them and had picked up nothing on their radars. Then, only thirty miles from the safety of Gibraltar, the *Ark* was unexpectedly struck amidships by a torpedo, fired from an undetected U-boat. There was a heavy explosion which lifted the ship and bounced the aircraft parked on the deck up in the air, a huge tower of spray shooting high above the tall carrier on the starboard side, the area under the bridge flooding with water straight away, the *Ark* immediately listing some 10 degrees. There was considerable confusion at first, as all internal communications had been severed. The captain, alarmed to see his radio masts horizontal instead of vertical and almost touching the sea, made the swift decision to abandon ship.

The naval historian William Jameson has given a graphic account of the last moments of the third *Ark Royal*:

Most of the Ark Royals were in the clothes they stood up in, but some had seized particularly treasured possessions. The pockets of a Petty Officer were bulging with silk stockings, presents for his wife. One of the ship's cats - a large ginger tom - arrived in the arms of a Royal Marine. Paymaster-Commander Steele had two suitcases full of money - £10,000 in each, it was said - and his appearance was greeted with a cheer. 'Schooly' Jenkin (Senior master) strolled up immaculately dressed, a folded raincoat over his arm and carrying a neat attaché case.

They had been travelling in a convoy, so a destroyer, *HMS Legion*, swiftly made its way to them. Hundreds waited on the port side of the *Ark's* lower hangar deck and further hundreds on the flight deck, as the destroyer cautiously approached. As soon as it came alongside, long ropes were let down, for even though the *Ark* was lurching on its side, it still towered above the *Legion*. Steam, pouring out from the boiler room's ventilation shafts, increased the sense of danger as the ship's company urgently began climbing down the ropes, hand over hand, David among them. He later wrote reassuringly to his parents:

The whole business was remarkable for its calmness and efficiency, considering the horrible angle of everything. When the flying and aircraft personnel left the ship, there was quite a jolly little regatta between the ship's side and the destroyer. The craft consisted of everything from cork mats to aircraft dinghies. My own exit was as dignified as could be expected in the circumstances! One chap, swimming away breaststroke, waved away a rope with 'No, no, I'm OK. See you in Gib!'

Thirteen hours later, the captain, his uniform green from the slime of the upturned carrier, slid into a tug and very soon the ship with all her contents, including David's Swordfish with its extra rear-view mirror and other 'home comforts', had disappeared for ever to its resting place 1,000 fathoms down. Next day, when the sun came up, the sea was completely calm. But for a large patch of oil and a certain amount of floating debris it was as if nothing untoward had occurred. On hundreds of past days, wrote William Jameson, this was the time when the *Ark* would be steaming fast into the wind, aircraft rising from her deck:

Waves underfoot and clouds overhead. Men at the guns watching the sky. Men on watch, men sleeping, men eating. Officers and ratings; young and old; wise and foolish; sad and gay; but all one company. All belonging. All conscious of something, which, like faith, is 'the substance of things hoped for, the evidence of things not seen'.

The loss of the *Ark Royal* was another blow to national morale at a most difficult time in the war. The newspapers strove to minimise the disaster, stressing that there were hardly any fatalities and nearly fifteen hundred survivors, and the *Daily Express* defiantly ran the front-page headline that ARK ROYAL WENT DOWN 'LIKE A GENTLEMAN'. But of course for the Carter and Nicholl families, as for so many others, news of the *Ark*'s sinking came as a terrible shock. It inevitably took time before a telegram from David arrived with the simple message 'Thanksgiving. Miraculous deliverance. All well.'

A little later, David was able to write to his parents more fully:

I do so hope you weren't too anxious, or, at least, not for long. I sent off a couple of telegrams at the earliest possible minute, but I'm afraid that at best they will not have reached you until well after the announcement of the loss of our ship.

I am now sitting in a most comfortable armchair on the balcony of a very nice hotel, overlooking Gibraltar harbour and bay. All is peace and quiet, which is very nice! It's funny how we all loved 'Old Ark' and we feel her loss much more even than our own possessions. Like most people, I only have what I stand up in. I had been flying during the morning, and so had nothing whatever in my pockets (except my *Daily Light* and a handkerchief-praise be!) I have already, however, bought a tie and collar (I was not standing up in those) - took them off in case the evacuation didn't go according to plan - and a toothbrush. I'm considering buying a pair of socks. My wristwatch is my only valuable left . . .

816 Squadron, which at one stroke had lost all its aircraft, was disbanded. Of the original pilots who had left Scotland in the *Furious* five months earlier, only David and one other now returned, all the others having been killed or invalided home suffering from stress-related illness. There was further tragedy too. Most of 816's current aircrew joined another squadron as a group, the ship to which they were attached shortly afterwards being blown up with total loss of life.

One immediate result for David of the sinking of the *Ark Royal* was the realisation of his hopes of spending Christmas at home on leave. These were precious days, spent partly with his parents at Reigate and partly at Ades with the Nicholls, where his growing affection for Jos's sister, Joanna, no doubt made him an even more regular visitor than usual. At 17, she was eight years his junior. Joanna herself many years later recalled:

David had always been a hero to me! He had always been so kind to the younger ones in the two families: myself, my younger sister Charitie and his own youngest sister Charlotte. He was never condescending with us, just loving and patient. One of my earliest memories was when I had my hair in plaits and David pulled them one day! But, to make up, he was driving his parents' Lanchester later and let me sit on his lap and steer the car. I must have been ten at the time.

The vivacious Joanna had often as a young girl surreptitiously tried to join in the holiday fun that her three elder brothers enjoyed with their Carter counterparts, making herself useful during their many games of tennis or squeezing into the dickey of David's Morris, 'Archie', or the back seat of his brother Stephen's old Humber, 'Henry', as they set off to the swimming pool. Her early birthday treats had sometimes included jaunts to London in 'Archie', and whenever the Carter-Nicholl brotherhood had gone to watch rugby at Twickenham, Joanna had always done her best to be included.

She was at boarding school when she heard of the sinking of *Ark Royal* and it was several hours before the news of David's safety arrived. Later, when she met him at Ades, she found him unaltered, at least superficially, and just as cheerful and modest as ever.

But he was a maturer, more thoughtful personality after his service in the *Ark*, and, as I soon discovered, had developed a much deeper spiritual life.

David and Joanna at the Nicholl's Sussex home, Ades

David with his camera at Ades with Joanna (r.), her mother, her sister Charitie
and her brother Geoff

# 5

# JOS AND HOPE

Jos was still languishing in Warwickshire at the time of the sinking of the *Ark Royal*, and a few weeks later, in December 1941, was transferred to a new Artillery battery with headquarters in the village of Bodicote near Banbury. The guns of Jos's latest battery were almost certainly protecting a large aluminium factory supplying the aircraft industry and employing a workforce of 4,000, thought so likely a target for enemy bombers that it was heavily camouflaged and a dummy factory built nearby to divert Luftwaffe attention.

Jos, in Royal Artillery uniform, on leave with his family at Ades

David and Jos met up with each other that Christmas, when both happened to be in Sussex on leave. Part of their reunion involved a theatre matinée in London which Jos organised for his own family and "dear David and any other particles of the Carter ensemble". David was expecting a posting abroad, and entrusted 'Archie' to Jos in his absence. Back in Bodicote, Jos wrote home:

I do feel ashamed to call myself in the Army, and now to be borrowing dear David's wizard bus – it's just too bad! But how sweet and typical of him to remember about the extra petrol ration.

Jos's early days at Banbury were enlivened by a sudden sighting of King George VI:

He came walking up the hill, inspecting the men on the side of the road while I stood on the other. I was so eagerly watching his actions and noting his style in riding breeches and field boots that I clean forgot to salute! However, I was able to rectify that when he came sailing past in the Royal Car ten minutes later!

And there were other occasional excitements. One letter, for example, tells how "Yesterday I actually piloted a Wellington!" Stationed not far from the Croughton RAF base, he had somehow managed to persuade a friendly young Squadron Leader to take him up, in the 2nd pilot's seat, in a bomber "which had been on both the early 1000 Bomber raids on Germany" and was now carrying out a routine test.

We went over some of our Artillery sites and I took over for a bit just before we got to Oxford. It was just grand to see the colleges and churches from the air. (Cambridge of course must look much better, but it was the next best thing!) I wasn't sick this time, chiefly because I was watching the controls whenever we banked and I knew what was going to happen . . .

Jos was by now more or less resigned to his inglorious lot of manning searchlights amid the placid fields of Oxfordshire – there had been no raids on Banbury and none seemed imminent – when, in April 1942, a sudden, personal setback rekindled his old desire to be a commando.

Two years earlier, when he had come back to Queens' College from a game of tennis to learn of its immediate closure, he had been accompanied by his mixed doubles partner, Hope Parry, a Bedford College student who had been evacuated from London to Cambridge at the beginning of the war. She and Jos had met when sharing a hymn - book in the crowded gallery of Holy Trinity Church. He had noted at once her sparkling eyes, and they were soon to discover they had much in common.

Hope, like Jos, came from two generations of missionaries, her grandfather having worked for the legendary Hudson Taylor, whose fifty-year ministry in China was said to have led to nearly 20,000 conversions. She herself had been born in remote north-west China, where her father was a doctor in a leprosy hospital. Hope's gentle yet single-minded personality neatly complemented Jos's more ebullient one. They had kept in touch after Jos was called up and the friendship flourished. In early 1942, Jos spent a 48-hour leave in Cambridge specifically to see Hope, and shortly afterwards she was invited for a weekend at his Sussex home, Ades. This was clearly an event of great importance to Jos who anxiously warned his parents that it could be quite an ordeal "facing practically the entire Nicholl family at a sitting". The following week, back amid the searchlights in the Oxfordshire countryside, Jos was quick to thank his parents for "the simply grand welcome" they had given Hope:

She thoroughly enjoyed it - despite the hilarity and jests that are synonymous with a true Nicholl welcome! Poppa, you were just grand (except at the very end!). Your restraint was admirable! Sussex absolutely rose to the occasion and what an occasion! . . . I just have to try to settle down to this life again in the meantime - and what a strain that is - particularly in view of the immediate past and the prospect of the immediate future . . .

Everything in Jos's life seemed perfect. Even the frustrations of the searchlights had momentarily receded. But not long afterwards all the euphoria suddenly evaporated when Jos, having rushed to Cambridge on his next leave to propose to Hope, was turned down. It was an eminently sensible decision, and no doubt very gently spoken. Both were only 21. The war would surely separate them, and even after it was eventually over, Jos would have to return to college to complete his degree. Hope, meanwhile, was only halfway through her own course. Jos, however, was absolutely devastated, later recalling that, at the moment of refusal, "the dim street lamp at the corner of Barton Road had started to sway". "If you won't marry me, Hope," he protested, "I'll go and join the Commandos!"

The worst of the storm soon blew over. A week later, he was able to write calmly to his parents:

Thank you so much for all your letters. Sorry I haven't written before, but I thought it better to get things straightened out in my own mind first. 'Things' are OK on all fronts now – tension relaxed, experience gained and one Jordan at any rate passed . . .

But, without telling his parents, he began seeking the whereabouts of Colonel Jack Churchill. If only he could engage the dynamic Churchill's support, he realised, strings might be pulled, red tape ignored, doors opened, and his bold assertion to Hope vindicated. As the summer of 1942 arrived, he began plotting his release from searchlights with the same unswerving determination he always showed on the games field. The ball was in his hands. Now, head down, he must run with it.

# 6

# DAVID: THE BATTLE OF COLOMBO

David had returned to his unit in January 1942 in positive mood, and, en route to Scotland, used a brief break at St Pancras station to dash off a quick note to his parents, which he ended with a verse from a hymn he had recently "appropriated" for his current needs:

We go in faith, our own great weakness feeling
And needing more each day thy grace to know,
Yet from our hearts, a song of triumph pealing;
We rest on Thee, and in Thy name we go.

Initially David was told he was joining an emergency force being hastily put together to defend key bases in the Far East. But this plan was aborted when, in February 1942, Singapore fell to the Japanese, and, instead, David was re-routed to Sri Lanka (then the British colony of Ceylon), which was thought to be similarly vulnerable. Going east was not the posting he had really wanted. He had hoped to join some friends in a squadron of Swordfish which was being assembled to make a heroic (and, as it was to prove, very costly) attack on the German battlecruisers *Scharnhorst*, *Gneisenau* and *Prinz Eugen*.

Nonetheless, as David travelled from England to India on board *HMS Lanka*, he felt relaxed and much refreshed from his leave, which no doubt helped him cope with the overcrowding and the sharing of a cabin, designed for two, with eight others. The seas were dangerous, the voyage tediously long and morale not generally high. Reports from nearly all theatres of war were gloomy in the early days of 1942. Japanese successes seemed relentless in the east, and America had only just entered the war. David told his parents:

The news since this journey began has been consistently bad. I find that I am too inclined to deserve the rebuke which Our Lord gave to Peter when "he saw the wind boisterous" instead of looking on Him. Of all times, now is the time to "look up".

On the *Lanka*, for the first time since joining the Navy, David found a few fellow Christians, and reported back to his parents that one of the things they had discussed was the joy of the Christian gospel, "in spite of the circumstances which caused Our Lord to be called a man of sorrows". And, fortified by this fellowship, David lost his earlier diffidence:

Our Father knows exactly what special encouragement is needed and he has given me this ... There are greater opportunities for witness than before. For one thing, we do find, even in the Navy, that ex-Ark people are quite celebrities. I do pray that I may not mis-use this is any way.

"My cup runneth over," he declared in another letter home, and so exuberant were his spirits that he later felt the need to explain things more fully:

I think I spoke in my last letter of the 'fun' I was having. On second thoughts, that was probably the wrong word. It gives the impression that one is heedless of the terrible things which are happening around me and all over the world; of the awful situation of the world now; or even that one is callous about having left you all at home. On the contrary, the leisure of this trip has given me the opportunity to realise all these things particularly vividly. It has also, though, given me the chance to enjoy those 'joys' (that's the word!) which God longs to give us ...

When they reached Bombay, David's initial pleasure in the freedom from the cramped conditions was tempered by his shock at the city's squalor and, worse, the seeming indifference of the British authorities and British servicemen towards it. The notes he jotted down at the time were uncharacteristically angry:

A few hotels, sometimes lavish, sometimes luxurious, sometimes tawdry, occasionally good, always expensive. A few European shops and a few wide streets. Surprisingly quickly, the quality of the shops on these main streets drops off. So does its tidiness and cleanliness. In fact, if you're not very careful, you're in danger of suddenly finding yourself in the 'native quarter'. Mind you, to turn off the main street is even more foolish–you're 'in it' right away.

But it's all right! As we come ashore, our minds with charming unanimity are fixed on the Grand, the Splendide or the Metropolitan. Certainly we'll want to know something about the organisation of this 'dump' if there's not a gin and lime immediately available. 'Hey, what are you having? Right! Three JCs, boy! What? Fifty *each*? Well, cheers!'

Soon after these unsettling experiences, David completed his journey east in another troopship, a converted liner, the *Stirling Castle*, in which he eventually arrived, in March 1942, at China Bay, Ceylon.

He found himself in a highly volatile situation. The Japanese, with their overwhelming air and sea power, had now overrun the Dutch East Indies, Siam, all British Malaya and southern Burma. David had been sent to Ceylon because, with its fine two harbours of Colombo and Trincomalee, the island offered the Allies the best possible base from which to defend India and its ocean. It was vital to allied strategy that Ceylon did not fall to the Japanese. Winston Churchill later wrote:

Energetic and almost frantic efforts were made by us to procure a sufficient force of fighting aircraft for the island before the expected Japanese attack.

And when the *Stirling Castle* arrived in Colombo, all efforts were certainly energetic and frantic. Intelligence sources told of a huge Japanese armada heading that way under General Nagumo, the same man who had led the attack on Pearl Harbour. There was a real danger that he would arrive too soon for the Allies. Only 48 hours before the attack was actually delivered, the harbour was still an easy target, completely filled with shipping, much of it from fallen possessions in the east. David later wrote of ships "strung like sausages across the harbour", and his own *Stirling Castle* was one of a dozen huge vessels having to wait a considerable time to get into port.

Eventually room was made and some priority was given to getting the Fleet Air Arm's baggage off. First they were lowered some seventy feet by the ship's derrick onto little vessels, lighters, which were bobbing up and down beneath the liner in the gathering dusk. David's lighter then fought its way through a melée of similar vessels until they reached the landing - stage where all was noise and confusion. It was totally dark by the time they reached the RAF's China Bay aerodrome (at the seaside resort on Ceylon's east coast, Trincomalee) and David was relieved to discover that a surprisingly high proportion of their party's baggage had been salvaged.

As Divisional Officer to the hastily assembled squadron, he was only too aware how random everything was after the orderliness of the *Ark Royal*. Some of the men under him had come from evacuated stations, others from sunk ships. Several had no papers at all. Understandably, in the rushed preparations for the island's defence, there were no chaplains or church parades, and David found that it was up to himself to fill the gap. "It looks," he wrote to his parents, asking for their prayers, "as if it might be an unparalleled opportunity."

China Bay gave David his first experience of the tropics. It was swelteringly hot. The darkness and noises at night were a surprise. The primitive aerodrome with its baked - mud runways and thatched huts was inhabited by fireflies, crickets, frogs and snakes. David's cabin had mosquito nets instead of windows, but, even so, unwelcome visitors were common. An enormous beetle, one night, penetrated the netting:

I suddenly saw it in the corner, but at that moment it saw me too and before I could reach for my revolver it came flying across the room! After several unsuccessful attempts I shot it down - it was an enormous great twin - engined job - with a gym shoe.

Rumours were rife about a likely Japanese invasion of the island. The RAF handed over to the Navy every available Swordfish, about 20, but unfortunately only a few of these were actually air - worthy. None was equipped for dropping torpedoes. Gradually, however, bits and pieces were found and 6 operationally serviceable aircraft were produced from the cannibalisation of the others and soon they were up in the air making practice attacks on the British flagship The crews were as makeshift as the aircraft. Some had been on their way to Singapore, others on their way back. Only one aircraft had a three - man team. One pilot was completely on his own, the others were one man short. David himself had an air-gunner but no observer. The RAF, by contrast, with their more modern equipment (which was still, at this stage of the war, denied the Fleet Air Arm) had managed to assemble at Colombo quite a powerful force. Winston Churchill declared:

By the end of March the position at Colombo was decidedly more secure. After all our efforts we had gathered about 60 serviceable fighters and a small short-range force of bombers.

The Battle of Colombo took place a little later than intelligence sources suggested it would. On 31 March 1942 defence forces on the island were at the ready, and so too was the British fleet under Admiral Somerville, south of Ceylon. For 3 days nothing happened. With some of his ships in need of water, Somerville, believing that the Japanese were no longer coming, withdrew to his base 600 miles away. No sooner was he there than a flying-boat on patrol sighted large enemy forces approaching Ceylon. The original warning had been correct in all but the timing.

Just before 8 o'clock on Easter Sunday morning, 80 Japanese dive-bombers from Nagumo's aircraft-carriers struck Colombo. Churchill later wrote:

All was ready. 21 of the attacking aircraft were destroyed at the cost of 19 of our own fighters and 6 Swordfish of the Fleet Air Arm in tense air combat. By 9.30 a.m. the action ceased.

David's 6 Swordfish had been given the impossible job of attacking the Japanese aircraft-carriers with torpedoes. These carriers were all recently built and fitted with the latest in anti-aircraft guns. The Japanese aircraft likewise were new and technically advanced, in strong contrast to the ancient Swordfish. It was not surprising, therefore, that the 6 Swordfish were all numbered among the allied losses.

All through their short period of pre-battle training, in the approach to Easter, the Fleet Air Arm crews knew that theirs would be something of a suicide mission. On 4 April, the night before the battle, rumours of the approach of the Japanese had become very intense and David's little squadron worked particularly late, determined to be as well prepared as possible. David wrote later:

We knew we were in for it in a big way. The outlook was very black. We didn't turn in till 12.15 a.m. Torpedoes and all the equipment we had were as ready as they ever would be. I remember walking up and down alone in the hangar, as work was proceeding at the far end; the darkness, where I stood, broken only by the light reflected from the machinery and the men working under the arc-lamp in the corner; and the silence: the only sound was the escaping air, as they changed and tested the torpedoes. I remember that I prayed then. The shadows were so dark. 'Thy will be done.' I remember also that I snatched a look at my *Daily Light* before I went to sleep: 'When my spirit was overwhelmed within me, then Thou knewest my path. He knoweth the way I take ...'

The next day started early. By 7.30 the 6 aircraft, loaded with torpedoes, were in the air, approaching the temporary aerodrome at Colombo racecourse, where they were expecting to land and refuel before taking off again to attack the carriers, said to be approaching. However, the arrival of David's squadron, in line-astern formation as they flew through a hastily raised balloon barrage, exactly coincided with that of the formidable Japanese air-fleet. A host of Japanese Zero fighters, probably mistaking David's squadron for RAF fighters climbing up to attack their bombers, came dashing down, guns blazing. With the advantage of height, speed and number (3-1), it did not take them long to shoot down the Swordfish, but it was long enough, as it later transpired, to allow the RAF squadrons, soon to arrive, to gain an important height advantage.

David saw very little of what happened to the other Swordfish, "except for one which, out of the corner of my eye, I saw go straight down in flames". This was the swordfish of Tony Beale DSC, a gallant 21-year-old pilot whose torpedo had struck the *Bismarck* amidships and crippled her, less than a year before. David was at 800 feet when he was attacked from above. One wing was hit and some bullets went through his instrument panel, but the aircraft's handling was largely unimpaired. He successfully eluded a second attack, but lost a great deal of height as he did so. Finally, in trying to avoid two Japanese fighters, he failed to see a third, which opened fire on him. His goggles were shot off his face, his instrument panel smashed, the tail-plane and elevators damaged, and, at about 50 feet above the water, the Swordfish became uncontrollable and smashed into the sea, fortunately at a fairly gentle angle and on a moderately even keel. It was, nonetheless, "a very sudden stop indeed".

The aircraft began to sink, very quickly, by the tail. David and his air-gunner, David Burns, somehow extracted themselves from their cockpits, David helping his air-gunner with the inflation of his life jacket, for he was badly hurt. With relief David watched as the emergency dinghy inflated perfectly and soon he and Burns were in the water holding onto the rope around the dinghy, David spending anxious moments trying to free the dinghy from the sinking craft, while air escaping from a torpedo was hissing alarmingly.

At last the dinghy was freed. I then noticed that my companion looked terribly bad. The Japs visible were now further away so I got in the dinghy. It took absolutely all my strength to haul David Burns in too. And then I saw what had happened. A cannon shell must have exploded very near his back and it was obviously a fatal wound. He became unconscious when he had only been in the dinghy a moment or two, but recovered, just for a moment, before he died. 'It's all going dark. It's all going dark.' Such an extraordinary urge to hold and support him in that moment was gripping me, but my support was human and weak. Perhaps at that moment, though, he knew the support of the Everlasting Arms . . .

David looked around him. He had drifted clear of the aircraft of which only the tip of one wing was still showing. The shore appeared to be a long distance away, perhaps 3 or 4 miles. He was just looking for some paddles when he heard a noise rise above that of the guns and bombs at Colombo. A Japanese aircraft was coming straight at him, at a menacingly shallow angle. Several had previously dived at him when he had first climbed into the dinghy, but this approach was distinctly different.

As the spurts of water from the bullets came rushing towards me, I was over the side and into the water. Then I tried to get down, and I had the impression that I got several feet below the surface. Probably, though, having an inflated life-jacket, I had deceived myself. It's funny, though, that in spite of thinking myself well down, I was certain that this was the end. And with that thought I remember praying 'God, forgive us for making this war inevitable by our own selfishness, and, God, forgive these men for trying to kill me'.

But I wasn't hit. Nor, miraculously, was the dinghy. When I surfaced, the plane was climbing away. I was visited by several more and each time I dived over the side, but I don't think any more opened fire. Before long, they had all gone for good. The gunfire over Colombo also stopped. A pall of black smoke was rising.

Back in the dinghy, he slowly paddled himself and his dead air-gunner towards the shore.

I prayed again. Prayed for parents who have lost sons. Partly thinking, I suppose, about my companion's parents and partly about my own, in view of my narrow escape.

Suddenly the beach was much closer and full of people, seemingly thousands of them. He had hoped to see a boat put out, but none came, so, although in shock and close to exhaustion, he dived into the water and pulled the dinghy behind him, hoping this might provoke a reaction. It did, for these were shark-infested waters. Two locals at once put out in a primitive version of a catamaran. David gratefully scrambled on board, and they towed in the dinghy, many friendly hands helping pull it through the surf, over the rocks and onto the dry sand beyond. A white-robed figure came forward from massed crowds. "We need your help," he told David. Just behind, David Burns' body was being lifted from the dinghy. He was laid on the hot, firm sand. "We need your help," the white-robed priest was repeating. He spoke immaculate English. He would arrange care of the body, he said, in the cloister of his church. In the meantime he asked David whether he would have a look at a plane further up the beach and two big bombs.

David dazedly complied. The bombs turned out to be a torpedo broken in two. So he marked off a large section of the beach 'Out of Bounds' and proceeded on a borrowed bicycle to the crashed Swordfish. This was on its nose and had a good number of holes in it. The village headman, who undertook its care, said the crew had been taken off in an ambulance.

David was then taken to a native hut where he was given hot coffee, milk out of a coconut, a pair of shorts, a shirt and sandals. The Roman

Catholic priest excused himself, his Easter Sunday morning service being already an hour behind schedule. Later, David went along to the Church and sat at the back:

It was a huge place and I retain an impression of a glory of red and gold, and figures clothed in white. In fact, I had to pinch myself to make sure they weren't angels! But then for the first time I was able to relax and thank my Father again for his mercies.

After the service and a late breakfast with the priest, David was collected by an ambulance and taken to the Australian Red Cross Hospital 10 miles away. En route they stopped by the beach to examine the wreckage of another Swordfish, which David recognised as the third member of his flight. The aircraft was very badly damaged, its skeleton lying half in the water, upside down.

At the hospital David was dabbed with iodine where a bullet had grazed the left side of his face and another his right forearm. He was persuaded to lie down, but within minutes he was on his feet, determined to report to his H.Q. in case the Japanese returned. Unable to make contact, he left the hospital, ignoring all protestations, and hitched a lift in a lorry back to Colombo where he spoke to the Commodore, the Admiral and even the C-in-C himself in the deep underground naval headquarters.

The allies were bracing themselves for another attack, but it never came, for the Japanese had decided to withdraw. Churchill summarised:

They were making a raid and a demonstration. If, of course, they had found Colombo unprepared and devoid of air defence, they might have converted their reconnaissance in force into a major operation . . . The stubborn resistance encountered at Colombo convinced the Japanese that further prizes would be dearly bought. The losses they had suffered in aircraft convinced them that they had come into contact with bone.

As usual David was careful to minimise parental anxieties, and of the events of Easter 1942 he simply said, "I have had a trying spell from which I emerged somewhat over-tired and have accordingly been granted some sick leave". But when he received a letter from his mother in which she mentioned feeling a special urgency to pray on his behalf that Easter Sunday, he wrote back, giving a few details. Even so, there was no indication of what his diary revealed: post-battle trauma of nightmarish intensity, a period of great physical and spiritual trial.

In the immediate aftermath of the battle came visits to hospitals, for which David had volunteered, but which he dreaded. Two of his friends, for example, were in terrible pain:

One had shocking face wounds, his whole jaw having been practically shot away. The other was in great agony of mind as to whether he would lose his leg or not, and it was almost a relief to him when they finally carried out the amputation.

There were also taxing hospital visits in Colombo, to visit seriously injured survivors of the sinking of the aircraft-carrier *Hermes* off Ceylon in the aftermath of the air battle. Of four close friends in the *Hermes* three had been killed.

Delayed shock took many forms. One day he was overtaken by a sudden tiredness when visiting some friends in Colombo:

I set off for home but suddenly realised I'd forgotten where I was going. With a tremendous effort of concentration I just managed to return to my friends' house.

Similarly, the first time he travelled by air after the battle, he became very distressed. He was only being flown a short distance to the aerodrome at Trincomalee to salvage what remained of his possessions, yet he identified some high-flying birds as Japanese fighters and, on landing, was convinced that the plane was going too fast. His vision, too, was affected, particularly in poor light, and the lush green lawns of Colombo appeared a disconcerting blue. Sometimes he felt so weak that he even struggled to pick up a tennis racket.

As he brooded on the deaths and injuries of many friends, he was subjected to a period of great spiritual turmoil. Years later he recalled in his diary memories of this second battle of Colombo and the strengthening of his faith which emerged from its testing:

Remember that phase of total doubting. How helpless and undermined you felt. How you came to the point, however, where you saw it was impossible to believe that there was 'nothing behind life', 'life has no meaning', 'life snuffs out at death' (these being the conclusions you had to reach if your 'highest god' was man's mind and achievements). All the disbelief ('How can there be a God of love with such great suffering in the world?') eventually became more difficult to maintain than the belief that life was a meaningful struggle between huge forces of good and evil; that behind life are forces that are tremendously real, even if your finite mind cannot grasp them or your physical senses touch them ... At this point you began to experiment again. You began to assume that these forces existed. You began to call the good ones 'God' and 'Father', as Jesus had done. You came to see that life, grasped in the way that Jesus demonstrated, is infinitely more worthwhile in itself and is a training for a further life of contact with God and more complete enjoyment and understanding of people and experiences we have known, loved and enjoyed in this life ...

As he emerged from this period of black doubts, he was helped in his physical recovery by a family friend who was working in Ceylon as a government agent and able to offer him some restful days in the coolness of the hills at Candy away from the heat of Colombo. Later the same friend took him on one of his regular circuits of the island, enabling him to enjoy wild, beautiful country. He visited tea plantations, a new irrigation project and a colonisation scheme as well as the lovely gardens of Peradinnja and Nuwara Eliyer. It proved immensely therapeutic.

Only three weeks after being shot down, David was ready to go on a new posting in East Africa, even though he was not yet allowed to resume flying. And, most auspiciously, on the quayside at Colombo, just prior to his departure, he suddenly came face to face with a friend from his Cambridge days. ("It was a tremendous joy, a touch with home. We both felt very strongly that it was a most loving gift from our Father.") As he sailed out of Colombo harbour, he wrote to his parents:

The news is hard now. Our Lord's return is the only final answer. I feel sure that he expects us to work, pray and fight faithfully.

The Battle of Colombo, with its confused aftermath, was a turning-point in David's life. He was to liken the Easter Sunday of 1942 to the day of his conversion:

There is only one other point in my life which stands out with comparable clearness. That was when I was 11 years old and my young mind first responded to the call of the Divine Master. Some seem to proceed more evenly along the Christian path than others. My progress has been very jerky, but I like to think that my time in Colombo was another step forward on the Christian path.

# 7

# JOS: PURSUING THE COMMANDOS

Unlike the Fleet Air Arm or the Royal Artillery, the Commandos, for all their distinctive green berets, had little history behind them. Although the term 'commando' dated back to the guerrilla warfare so successfully employed by the Boers forty years earlier, the idea of utilising Special Service Commandos for making unexpected raids on an enemy's coastline was only first adopted by the British Army at the Prime Minister's instigation in 1940. Churchill astutely realised that commando raids could be not only strategically valuable but also good for public morale in hard times. 3 Commando and 2 Commando, the units Jos was currently actively pursuing, had featured within the last twelve months in two much-publicised raids (on the Norwegian port of Viragos and the Nazi-held French docks at St. Nazaire), which very much exemplified their levels of selfless bravery. The self-sacrificial ethos of the commandos was well summarised by one survivor in 1945:

Our peculiar fighting tradition could only have been born in a backs-to-the-wall era like 1940. It was simply this: that you went into action not as part of a properly equipped army but on your own, and with what you had and could carry, and without support and supply. And when you did so, you wrote yourself off at the start. If you came back, it was a windfall, a bonus, worth an extra point. If you didn't come back, then someone on the other side had found it expensive. Of course this view was a bit too melodramatic to express, so we hid it behind a great display of blanco and bright buckles and a parade ground drill we borrowed from the Guards . . .
(Colonel Robert Henriques)

Jos's campaign to defeat Royal Artillery red tape involved going to the very top. He had managed to acquire a letter of support from the dashing John Durnford Taylor, who had formed Britain's first commando unit (3 Commando) and personally led the attack on Viragos and several other equally dangerous targets. "I have investigated his credentials," wrote Durnford Taylor, "which appear to be good. I should like him attached, pending posting . . ." Posting, alas, was still not forthcoming, but in the meantime Jos was on the trail of Jack Churchill's two most trusted deputies at 2 Commando: the adjutant, Major Harry Blissett, and the second-in-command, the Duke of Wellington, a thirty-year-old regular officer, whom Jos had never met but, as the Earl of Mornington, had been a pupil at Stowe a few years before Jos. In late July 1942, having been promised an interview, Jos had made the difficult journey from Banbury to an Infantry Training Centre near Bury St Edmunds only to learn that both Blissett and the Duke had moved on to London, where they might be found either at Lord Mountbatten's Combined Operations headquarters in Whitehall, or at the Duke of Wellington's London home, Apsley House. Jos doggedly found his way to war-torn Piccadilly and approached the pillared portico of Apsley House. The doorbell echoed in the dim recesses of the servants' quarters, and after what seemed an interminable wait, an inscrutable butler opened the door. "Could I speak to Captain Blissett?" asked Jos. "Captain Blissett," replied the butler slowly, "has left with his Grace by the night train for Scotland." The chase was over. Jos's leave had expired and such a journey was impossible.

Many might thereupon have given up the unequal struggle. But not Jos. His next leave found him travelling by train to Glasgow and from there to Ayr, where he had at last tracked down his quarries to their Scottish lair. It was a big moment:

As I walked down the side of Wellington Square, I could tell 2 Commando's H.Q. easily enough from its immaculately attired sentry with fixed bayonet, who saluted as I approached. There was an even more resplendent figure at the head of the steps. He had a collar and tie and sported a magnificent moustache. Dutifully I saluted him and asked to see the Adjutant. From his position the figure looked down at me. 'He is inside . . . . Sir.' With horror I looked at his forearm and saw I was speaking to the Regimental Sergeant-Major . . .

Jos was taken along a bare passage and into an almost deserted room. There were just two figures, the very two he had so long been seeking: Harry Blissett, a bluff ex-schoolmaster now Adjutant of 2 Commando, was sitting behind a desk which he dwarfed; and, standing behind him, another Captain, soon to be one of Jos's most valued friends, Henry Valerian George Wellesley, the sixth Duke of Wellington, usually known as 'Morny'. The walls of the room were blank except for one composite picture, made up of passport photos of the twenty-two officers who had participated in the St. Nazaire raid, nineteen of whom were now either dead or prisoners-of-war. Jos read the names, fascinated, one by one: Lt. Col. Newman, VC, P.O.W., Major W. Coland, DSO, P.O.W . . . . Each interviewee, Jos later discovered, was shown these photographs as his first test. Fortunately for Jos, he had exhibited awe and admiration in equal measure, whereas several would-be commandos had simply turned very pale.

He was next shown into what seemed "a small cubby-hole leading off the Adjutant's office", and there was the man who had first given him hope that one day he might become a commando, John Malcolm Thorpe Fleming 'Jack' Churchill. Now in his mid-thirties, a Sandhurst-trained regular soldier, toughened in Burma, Churchill had also been a newspaper editor, and, thanks to his talent for archery, had once appeared in *The Thief of Bagdad* with Douglas Fairbanks and Anna May Wong. Using this very same talent on a commando raid in occupied France in 1940, 'Mad' Jack had famously felled a sentry with a perfect shot from his longbow. Soon afterwards, on another raid, in Norway, where he won the MC, he had played *The March of the Cameron Men* on his bagpipes as he jumped out of the leading landing craft, before nonchalantly lobbing a grenade at, and charging towards, a formidable Nazi gun emplacement.

For the first time, I was confronted by 'Mad' Jack Churchill. I can remember little of that bizarre interview. After some vague remarks about our correspondence, with some desultory replies and desperate hesitation on my part, Jack asked me if I was an archer. Much as I wanted to say 'Yes' to everything, I had to admit I wasn't. So I received a brief lecture complete with demonstration. Similarly I had to admit that I hadn't been in the habit of canoeing, another subject 'Mad' Jack enthusiastically expatiated upon. The interview seemed to be going all the wrong way . . .

Worse was to come. After commenting that they didn't usually accept officers wearing spectacles, 'Mad' Jack ushered Jos along to a survivor from St. Nazaire, the Medical Officer, Captain Mike Barling. It was only later that Jos realised that this eye test was really a character assessment. "Get out the sight card, Corporal Simister!" began the M.O.. As the corporal produced it, Jos desperately tried to read the top lines and learn them by heart, but the room's darkness wasn't helpful. "Oh, take it outside, Corporal!", said Barlow surprisingly. Jos sneaked a quick look at the next line as he did so. 'Well, now,' said Barlow, seemingly unsure where to place the card, "Let's find somewhere for it". As Jos was taking further furtive glances in its direction, the M.O. slowly looked around, eventually selected a ledge and methodically counted out ten paces. "OK, Nicholl," he declared at last. "Now, tell me, what you can see? And, oh, by the way, I think you'd better take off your glasses!" Jos successfully called out all the various lines of the card, completely from memory.

It had altogether been an odd interview at Ayr, not at all what he had expected, and as he hitched a lift back in the draughty interior of a Stirling bomber, Jos was convinced he would hear no more from 2 Commando. Instead, he was summoned back to the Ayrshire coast, one of 51 officers called to the Headquarters of the Special Service Brigade at Ardrossan and virtually the last to be interviewed. A panel of weary Senior Officers fired various questions at him. Finally, with apparent unconcern, they asked, "Tell us, Lieutenant Nicholl, why do you want to join the Commandos?"

It was hard to strike a happy medium between over-keenness and indifference. 'I want to see action,' I got out eventually. Little did I know that that was the only acceptable answer. Any 'I'm browned off with doing nothing', 'I don't see eye-to-eye with my Colonel' or 'I want promotion' was met with an immediate black mark and, whatever his other qualifications, that officer was rejected. Only long after, when I was doing the interviewing myself, did I appreciate the significance of the apparently innocent question and the crucial importance of the right answer.

In late August 1942 a wonderful telegram arrived. Jos was to report to Commando Depot, Achnacarry, Spean Bridge, Invernessshire within 48 hours. This time there was absolutely no opposition from the Searchlight

Battery. Strings had been pulled, red tape cut, prayers answered. Two years of deep frustration were at last over. The future, of course, was still uncertain. Several good young officers, he knew, had failed to come through the extreme challenges of the Achnacarry training programme. Yet, at long last, there was at least a very sporting chance that, against all the odds, he might yet make it as a commando.

# 8
# DAVID IN EAST AFRICA

In May 1942 David crossed the Indian Ocean to another important outpost of the embattled British empire, Kenya, where the British Eastern Fleet had retreated after the Japanese raid on Columbo, establishing itself at Kilindini, Mombasa's heavily fortified port. Having arrived at Kilindini, David discovered that the Fleet Air Arm was consolidating its position there by creating new aerodromes around that area. He was initially sent down to help the work going on at Port Reitz, ten miles to the south, before being given the job of setting up a completely new airfield at a village called Mackinnon Road, about fifty miles inland from Mombasa, deep in the Kenyan jungle.

The Mackinnon Road Fleet Air Arm base, which David helped build into a facility handling as many as 60 aircraft, began as little more than a small clearing for about half-a-dozen tents. He told his parents:

The camp is much frequented by snakes, ants and other insects, while beyond its perimeter roam lions, elephants, giraffes, ostriches, wild pigs and rhinosser-you-can-spell-them . . .

There was a one-track railway nearby, built back in late Victorian times to connect Mombasa with Nairobi and little altered since. A primitive road, which gave its name to the little settlement and had initially been constructed for ox carts, was of a similar vintage and offered a slow, bumpy drive to Kilindini. The village's most notable feature was the grave of Seyyid

Baghali, a railway worker of legendary piety and physical strength, much revered by Muslims, Hindus and Sikhs.

David was soon facing a number of small problems: the rationing and distribution of precious water supplies; the high-spirited antics of the local Mackinnon Road population (unexpectedly finding employment as cooks, servants, carpenters and labourers); and bringing his limited scientific knowledge to bear on the all-important, but regularly malfunctioning, camp wireless. Health was also a concern, with outbreaks of malaria and a sickness from the unpleasant 'jigger fleas' which attacked the feet. As the airfield quickly grew in size, David found the need to improvise off-duty activities for the growing number of ratings, some of whom he tutored for exams which might further their service careers. He made efforts, too, to break down the serious language barrier with the locals, though never managing more than a few words of their language and having to get by for much of the time with making signs. He also found himself organising and taking the Sunday services.

David at the Mackinnon Road base, 1942, with (l.-r.) Msee, Matthew Silas, Kikonu and Abdullah

There was only one other officer with him to share all the responsibility, a "dead-beat Lieutenant Commander", already court-martialled once, whose inept treatment of the ratings and locals appalled David. "I have never been so furiously angry with anyone in my life," he confessed in one letter home, but adding that the outburst, while having no effect on the recalcitrant officer, had probably been a valuable emotional outlet for himself. Likewise good came from bad when an aircraft in which he was flying as a passenger crashed very heavily, fortunately without major injuries or any loss of life. Strangely, this second crash seemed to remove the trauma of being shot down at Columbo, and very soon afterwards David was flying regularly again.

It took two months to create the Mackinnon Road airfield. When the job was finished, the locals were genuinely sad to see David go, particularly the man who had acted as his servant for the duration, and who, for his eight shillings a month, spent his time sitting inside, or lovingly polishing, David's official car. Large numbers of locals ran alongside the train, waving goodbye, as it slowly made its way out of the dilapidated station.

Back at Kilindini, David spent three months of further training, familiarising himself with several types of aircraft more modern than the Swordfish, and took over command of a squadron being readied for active service. Even at Kilindini conditions were far from easy, much equipment having to be improvised and much initiative therefore needed.

As he spent his days trying to ready his planes and crew, he found his moods fluctuating alarmingly:

Every other day I come to the conclusion that I am completely incompetent and entirely useless. On the days between I am inordinately pleased with myself. All this inconsistency is a horrible thing in a Christian . . .

During this training period there was the occasional reminder of the ongoing war. One night, for example, David had the unnerving experience of being ambushed. He had been taking his squadron night flying from a recently created airstrip a few miles from the town of Tanga, and had stayed on to complete some paper work before driving back in a truck half-an-hour after the other members of his flight. It was not much of a road, just two wheel tracks, with jungle vegetation closing in on both sides. It was early morning, still very dark, though the sky could just be discerned above the silhouetted trees. Having rounded a bend, David suddenly became aware of a shadow thrown by his headlights against the vegetation ahead. Instinctively he began braking, and on catching sight of the shadow's source, a bar or rope, stretched taut across the road, level with the top of his bonnet, he stopped the truck in its tracks, the impact flinging him hard against the steering column.

Winded and not a little alarmed, David tried the driver's door only to find that it was jammed. The engine was still running, so he attempted to move forward in 1$^{st}$ gear. The truck was held fast and his spinning wheels effected nothing. David switched off the lights and engine, and listened.

I prayed too. The night was full of the usual tropical jungle sounds, principally crickets, and the gleam of many glow-worms. But I was principally looking over my shoulder through the truck, expecting to see the canvas back part, as someone climbed in. It was one of those trucks with a hard cab in front, its spare tyre on top and canvas-covered hoops behind. I hadn't been fired upon, so it was probable that any men waiting for me in the darkness only had knives. If so, I would be best off in the truck. What was holding the truck? The rope I'd seen had passed out of sight, so it must have lodged somewhere above the cab. I moved my head against the offside window and looked up. There it was, showing against the sky. I edged across to the nearside window. Sure enough, it was showing there too. Cautiously, I opened the window to feel it. Steel wire hawser, a little larger than a thumb. I tried to move it, but it was jammed above the cab. So I moved the truck back and the freed wire fell on the bonnet. I moved the cab forward and tried to lift the wire over the cab. I couldn't manage it. There was no alternative but to brave a knife in my back. The doors would open now, so I got out, gingerly, and manhandled the wire over the roof, moving the lorry forward by stages.

Clear at last, David was able to drive on and was soon safely running down on a wider stretch of road towards the lights of Tanga. Exactly *why* this ambush was prepared, David never learnt. Nor why the would-be ambushers took no action or were absent when he fell into the trap, so recently prepared. It was another entry in the growing catalogue of merciful escapes.

# 9
## JOS AT ACHNACARRY

Jos's month of commando training at Achnacarry in Scotland, in the late summer of 1942, was prefaced by a few initial days designed to weed out the weakest candidates straight away:

We had a pretty full week which included every sort of physical entertainment - from bayonet fighting to swimming in full kit. We had tests but no exams. I managed all the tests, except climbing a rope crossing a gap of 20 feet and climbing down a rope at the other end - in full kit! The endurance run consisted of a flat race in full kit - less rifle - of two miles . . . Then we had swimming 100 yards in denims - followed immediately by 2 minutes afloat and 25 yards in full kit (equipment and pack, steel helmet, rifle over the shoulder and boots tied to the rifle). Then climbing a 6ft wall without assistance and jumping a ditch of 8 ft 6 in. An alarm race - 100 yards with a complete change of clothing to be done in the middle - and another race, carrying a man of similar size and weight 120 yards in 2 minutes . . .

Jos loved the whole physical challenge, and it brought out his favourite adjective. This first week, he reported, was just "grand".

Achnacarry is a remote village deep in the highlands, about fifteen miles north of Fort William on an isthmus between two long lochs, not far from Ben Nevis. There, the Commandos (who never did things by halves) had taken over for their Depot Headquarters a baronial castle, which for the past 150 years had belonged to the Cameron Clan. The training programme was the brainchild of a vigorous veteran of the First World War, Commander

Charles Vaughan, and it achieved standards of courage, toughness and fitness which were probably unprecedented in the British Army.

Vaughan made maximum use of the nearby mountains and lochs in his punishing regime. There were no set hours, and except for some limited periods of sleep, training was continuous. New ideas, sometimes very zany, were regularly embraced to keep things fresh and unpredictable. During his month at Achnacarry Jos's activities included 'Unarmed Combat' (a violent form of judo); 'Opposed Landings' (with real tracer bullets from 'defending' machine guns - there was an unfortunate fatality on one such exercise while Jos was there); vigorous PE (always done stripped naked to the waist, regardless of weather); abseiling (down a 40-foot rope from the tower of the castle - a particularly hard ask for Jos who had no head for heights); 'Speed Marches' (15 miles in 3 hours, carrying rifles and bren guns); 'Grenade Confidence' (involving a brave pause after the removal of the pin); 'Me and My Pal' (2-man attacks with Tommy guns and grenades on tricky targets); the 'Toggle Rope Bridge'; the 'Death Slide'; and any number of night manoeuvres. The course also included cliff-climbing, seamanship, knowledge of high explosives, demolitions and sabotage and living solitarily under a bivouac for long periods. Rejoicing in his escape from the searchlights, Jos met all these challenges with relish. In one typical letter home he commented:

My particular squad is giving a demonstration of unarmed combat this morning! Then after lunch we have to give a demonstration attack on some pillboxes - more running about - but great fun.

There were no Health and Safety regulations in those days, no excessive guide-rules from a 'Nanny state' to temper the toughness of Charlie Vaughan's training programme. Nor was there any let-up. In his last week at Achnacarry, Jos had just led his men home from a daunting cross-country run to find that Vaughan had organised a boxing competition, in which each troop had to provide seven fighters, graded according to height and weight. A ring was set up around a patch of grass. Bouts lasted a minute, at the end of which Colonel Vaughan held up a green or red flag to signify the winner. Officers were expected to compete with their men, and so Jos, with no previous boxing experience, soon found himself face to face with a bulky ex-policeman:

With little idea of defence, I decided to rush in. A jab on the cheek knocked me back, but it was no good waiting to be hit, so in again I went, and the next thing I knew was this mighty policeman was standing over me, waiting for me to get up. After a few more pathetic flails, mercifully the round was over. Trying to look the part of a defeated hero, I went round to the cookhouse searching for a juicy steak.

He had only just found one when he learnt that his section had won through to the next round. By the time it took place, his eye was virtually closed. 'All ready!' grinned Colonel Vaughan, banging his gong, as Jos's second fight began. At the end of it, he was no longer anxious about the left eye, for the right one wouldn't open.

A day later, the training course ended. There was no formal Passing Out. Two or three participants were returned to their units on the grounds that they were insufficiently fit, and the rest had a week's leave before becoming fully-fledged commandos. His ambitions finally realised, in early October 1942 a delighted Jos joined 2 Commando to take responsibility for one of 5 Troop's two Sections. He must have been an awesome sight with his two black eyes.

# 10

# DAVID IN MADAGASCAR

David's five months in East Africa ended inauspiciously with two weeks in bed with fever and suspected malaria, but he wrote cheerfully soon afterwards that he was "flying again quite merrily" and "off on what may be a very interesting job". His new destination was the island of Madagascar, which, as a French colony, was now under the control of the pro-Nazi Vichy government. The worry was that Madagascar (which was larger than France itself) might offer its many fine harbours to the Japanese, whose long-range submarines might then do terrible damage to vital shipping routes, and, in particular, the 8th Army. Earlier, in May, at the same time as the Battle of Colombo, an allied amphibian operation involving 3 Commando had seized the most important and northern of all Madagascar's harbours, Diego Suarez (modern Antsiranana). Now it had been decided that the whole island should be captured, to discourage growing Japanese interest in it.

Hostilities were renewed on 8 September 1942 with an amphibious landing at Majunga (Mahajanga). On 10 and 11 September, while Jos was reaching the final two weeks of his commando training at Achnacarry, David's squadron of Fairey Fulmars (two-crew fighters, with a top speed of 270 mph, twice as fast as that of the Swordfish) flew across from Tanga to Majunga, a 7-hour flight involving a refuelling stop on a tiny island in the Indian Ocean. David found Madagascar, for all its colour and wild, natural beauty, strangely unsettling. Another British soldier, serving there at the same time as David, later wrote of it:

The first I saw of Madagascar was the eerie colour of its soil. It gave to the sky, the vegetation and the people a strangeness, even a deathliness, which still shadows my recollections of the island. For the soil and the dust which rose from it to cake our skins and clothes, our eyelids and nostrils, was not quite brick-coloured or terracotta but the colour of dried blood. Against it the vegetation seemed unnaturally stark and cactaceous while the brown skins of the inhabitants showed purple depths in hollow cheeks and eye-sockets . . . (Rupert Croft-Cooke, *The Blood-Red Island*)

The operation before David and his squadron was by no means straightforward. The Vichy government's forces included many conscripted locals, so for several weeks David and his crews were distributing leaflets, encouraging surrender, as they did reconnaissance work around important objectives like the capital Tananarive (Antananarivo), Fianarantsoa, Ambalavao and Ihosy. Surrender, unfortunately, did not happen - the Axis' propaganda proving the stronger - and so the fighting began as the Allies attempted to defeat and dislodge Madagascar's obstinate pro-Vichy leader, General Annet.

To begin with, David was stationed at Diego Suarez, his role to strafe specific targets with accuracy (the Fulmars had 8 wing-mounted machine-guns) and to maintain air cover for the troops below. It proved a short but bitter and confused campaign, fought mainly on the ground, with atrocities committed on both sides. Fleet Air Arm losses were alarming, the mountainous, heavily-forested island providing inhospitable country over which to fly. From one mission, led by David, only two planes returned out of a party of six.

In some ways, however, he found the open conflict somewhat more straightforward than the month of phoney war which had preceded it. "It is easier to shoot straight," he noted grimly, "than to carry out an accurate air reconnaissance." Nevertheless, it was an eerie war, fought out in front of an expectant, vulnerable local population, David's sorties often being watched by the Malgaches. The Allied High Command's restraint in the face of much provocation and a protracted campaign impressed David. He was impressed too by the restraint of the pilots:

I pray hourly that the fighting may stop, but I feel that while it is on it is a great thing that people who hate hurting others should be on this particular job, as we have the most formidable weapons and plenty of opportunity for using them . . .

Conditions during the Madagascan campaign were often most trying. Some of the airfields were nothing but bare spaces of wilderness, where supplies often failed to materialise. David learnt for the first time what real thirst was like when his squadron went without water for two days. (After dividing up their last supply - about a tablespoon each - he had walked three miles in blazing noonday heat in an unsuccessful attempt to locate some more.) Sometimes the only shelter from the fierce sun or wind was under the wings of the aircraft. There was a time, too, of near starvation, when a few tins of bullybeef were all his crews had to eat. Flies and ants, meanwhile, took possession of everything. There were extremes of temperature. In contrast to days of suffocating heat were nights of terrible cold. At one airfield at sea level David would lie awake at night, sweating, without a blanket; at another, the next night, at 5,000 feet, he would be shivering despite three blankets and his flying kit.

His letters home, as ever, tended to make the best of things:

I'm sitting now in a tent over 5,000 feet up, several miles from anywhere, the aerodrome just a flat place among the hills, and only *just* big enough for our fairly fast aeroplanes. Food is rather simple, but quite good. Unfortunately, our only naval rating cook is ill (with food poisoning!) and we have to put an electrician and an armourer on the job. Today, actually, the point is immaterial. All our cooking is done in the open air and today the rains have come! And evidently, when it rains here, there are no half measures about it. The noise on the canvas is too much for us to discuss the matter, so here we sit, pondering our next move and thinking of our next hot meal. Still, there is a bright side to everything! The tent next door has chosen this, of all opportunities, to collapse!

David's faith was again a source of great strength in coping with the distress of the death of friends in action, as well as innocent civilians. From the lovely city of Antsirabe, for example, he confided to his parents:

*Daily Light* this morning reminds me how much I owe to the psalms. Especially of late I have found them a wonderful source of comfort. It is most extraordinary how often I have really felt that I didn't want to fly any more, and just at that moment there always seems to come a break. Again and again such things make me marvel at God's love.

And, at around the same time:

God's care for me in physical matters fills me with a certainty that He will look after this part of my life too. It is something – no, everything – to have learnt that my only hope is in my Saviour. I wish I could describe the wonder of the love with which I have been brought through a very dark way this year. Even in retrospect the way looks as dark as ever. But I don't think that for a moment I have been allowed to doubt His presence. I think I have been borne along by your prayers, when I myself had become speechless.

There was one particular blessing. In arranging a memorial service for a member of his squadron, David had first met the Frisch family, Norwegian missionaries who ran the Lutheran church in Antsirabe (a city founded by Norwegian missionaries). Soon the Frisch's were organising regular services in English on Sunday mornings specially for David and his men. Marie Frisch wrote to David's parents:

It is really great to see all these fine young men and officers, with David at their head, coming to the services, taking such a real interest in them and singing out the hymns with such full voices.

David became a frequent guest at the Frisch home, heading there whenever he could on his recently acquired ex-French army motor-cycle, and was very soon one of the family. "We felt a real Christian fellowship binding us together," wrote Marie.

Madagascar was eventually captured after two months of fighting. The capital Tananarive fell early. Andriamanalina was taken on 18 October. Ambalavao followed. David's squadron was involved in various sorties, sometimes with strategic sites in towns as targets, sometimes Vichy aerodromes. When the Vichy Governor-General eventually surrendered near Ilhosy, in the south of the island on 8 November, the Allies' commanding officer, Brigadier General Dawson, wrote approvingly to David and his headquarters staff:

David (3rd from left) and one of his Fulmars, Antananarivo, November 1942, with (l.-r.) his fitter, armourer, observer Adrian Willson, rigger and electrician.

David with his squadron's senior observer, George Creese, in front of a Fairey Fulmar in which they led several sorties

Please accept for yourselves and convey to all ranks under your command my congratulations on the grand work that you have performed in the operations that terminated today. The great part you played is fully appreciated both by myself and the forward troops you supported so well. We all thank you and wish you every success in future ventures.

Three days later, in mid-November 1942, David's depleted squadron retraced its way back to the familiar surroundings of Kilindini and Mackinnon Road.

For all the horrors of the campaign, David took back with him high opinions of the island and its people. He loved the French atmosphere, with colourful little towns nestling in the hills, exuding Gallic charm. He admired the French cooking and enjoyed trying out his schoolboy French on the Malgaches, leading, on the strength of it, most of the parties which went shopping, scrounging or requisitioning. He was moved by the friendliness of the Malgaches and loved the plentiful fruit (notably the pineapples, at a penny each). He was impressed too by the ingenuity with which the locals faced their various shortages. There was, for example, no material available for clothes, so sackcloth was manufactured from a locally-grown sisal: "The French succeed in looking quite chic in it." Curtains were made out of sacking, and so acute was the shortage of paper and wood, that English matches were split into four pieces for re-use. Cars seemed to thrive on some form of sugar spirit, which was also drunk by the Malgaches in bars. Among all the distress and devastation of war, he took some comfort from the many indications of the human spirit flourishing bravely in adversity.

# 11
## JOS: COMMANDO IN WAITING

For a short while, in October 1942, it looked as if Jos and No. 2 Commando might be going into immediate action. Only a month earlier at Dieppe, 3 and 4 Commando had participated in a bold but costly amphibious raid, testing the effectiveness of the Nazi defences on the French coast, from which only 40% of the force returned to England, and when 2 Commando were rushed down to a Dorset camp to take part in a frenetic rehearsal of marine assaults, cliff-scaling and night manoeuvres, it seemed another big-scale testing of Nazi coastal defences was imminent. There was great disappointment when it was called off and 2 Commando returned to their Scottish base, Ayr.

Jos as a commando subaltern

The men in 2 Commando, around 300 in all, were recruited from many different military and social backgrounds. Each commando unit was subdivided into six Troops of 50 men (under the command of a Captain), and these in turn were split into two Sections (each under the command of a young subaltern). Jos's immediate job was to impose himself on his Section of 6 Troop, to which he had just been transferred, and he was soon leading them street-fighting in a demolished slum near Kilmarnock, cliff-climbing on the Heads of Ayr, field-firing at Dunoon and beach-assaulting (with grappling irons) on the promenade at night. The imminent arrival of a Brigadier in late January precipitated a two-hour parade in sleet and snow on the barrack square.

Jos would regularly liaise over the programme with the other Section-leader in his Troop, thirty-year-old Frank Mason, who soon became a good friend:

Frank was a family man who, as a commercial traveller, had knocked about the country quite a bit. Working up to Sergeant in an infantry regiment, he had been commissioned into the Reconniassance Corps. Dark, squat and swarthily handsome, he had a decided will of his own, which often came into conflict with our immediate boss, 6 Troop Leader, the fierce-looking Captain Dickie Hooper. But their differences were always only momentary and there was not the slightest animosity on either side.

Dickie Hooper was a short, dapper man with a trim moustache, who had not only won the MC at St Nazaire but also been one of the few to return. He was a keen sportsman ("Dickie certainly knows a thing or two about rugger") and always prepared to sing a song at Troop suppers. Jos was soon following his example, and as he was known as 'Joe' in the army, usually chose Stephen Foster's ballad 'Poor Old Joe'.

It was at Ayr that Jos first came into close contact with Mason's great friend John Jeffreys, a Section officer with 2 Troop. Billeted with Jos at the Berkeley Hotel, Mason and Jeffreys proved a boisterous pair who were very much the despair of the landlord.

John had a very different background from Frank. After Eton and Sandhurst, he had become a regular officer in the King's Own Scottish Borderers, and had gone out to France with the British Expeditionary Force. On his return, via Dunkirk, he had become dissatisfied with the inactivity of a staff existence, and, shortly after I did, he joined the commandos. Young-looking, tall with auburn hair and a most attractive stutter when he got worked up, John had a really wicked sense of humour ...

Jeffreys was always very reticent about his family, but his distinguished grandfather, Sir Roger Keyes, had been the Commandos' first Director of Combined Operations, and his cousin, Geoffrey Keyes, of 11 Commando, had just won a posthumous VC for landing 250 miles behind enemy lines in Africa and attacking Rommel's desert headquarters. John Jeffreys, clearly, had his cousin's pugnacity and loved the commando ethos. Scotland in January was not the ideal time for swimming in the ocean but, as Jos's letters reveal, Jeffreys had soon encouraged him to do so:

We had a grand bathe after a hard day on Wednesday & Thursday. The sun was shining and it really was no colder than Seaford in September. We felt we could knock a house down afterwards - but as for trying to swim 100 yards or so, I just couldn't do it. It's just like a cold bath - we run down to the beach to get warm, straight into the sea, duck in and out - and then run all the way back. Dicky Wake and John Jeffreys, who do it with me, are determined to bathe in every month of the year - they've only got February and March to go!

Now that he was a commando, Jos was so much more at ease with himself, scoring any number of tries in ad hoc games of rugby, and enthusiastically sharing in the developing camaraderie and the honing of physical skills. Like the other newcomers, he was of course desperate to see some action and prove himself. When news of an embarkation abroad eventually came, he shared the sense of relief which flooded through 2 Commando after so many months of training.

For David, by contrast, being abroad had long lost its initial excitement. And as Jos prepared for service in distant parts, David was nursing hopes that maybe, before long, after nearly a year away, an opportunity might soon arise for a return home ...

The officers of 2 Commando. Jos is second from right in the back row. 'Morny'
is seated third from left, with Jack Churchill fifth, Harry Blissett sixth, and Dickie
Hooper eighth from left.

# 12

# DAVID: RETURN FROM EAST AFRICA

While Jos had been plunging into icy Scottish waters, David had been marking time before his posting back to England with a short stay in the sultry heat of the Mackinnon Road airfield, which had grown considerably since he last knew it. Time lay strangely heavily there, and having discovered that there had been no form of religious service since his departure five and a half months previously, David at once applied himself to remedying the situation, his natural diffidence offset by the encouraging response his lead in Madagascar had elicited. "Please pray," he asked his parents, "not only that I may honour our Master by wise decisions and tactfulness, but that I may not dishonour him by relying on myself and failing."

Soon as many as 80 of the 130 Navy personnel on the base were crowding into a big marquee for the services. There was no piano, so singing was unaccompanied, and the shortage of typewriters meant that all the hymn sheets had to be copied out by hand. Sometimes there were big puddles of water inside the marquee, such was the force of the monsoon rain, and on one occasion 2 inches fell during a service:

I had to stand in the middle of the marquee to make myself heard. This was perhaps fortunate, as a snake, eight feet long, driven by the water and attracted by the lights, paid us a visit. It came in just behind where I 'ought' to have been standing. The men took a short 'stand-easy' while the matter was resolved, before the service recommenced.

David organised a somewhat less dramatic carol service shortly afterwards, but with an even better attendance of virtually everyone on the base, as well

as a large number of enthusiastic Africans crowding in at the back. The
direction of such well-subscribed but makeshift services, he confessed to his
parents, "made me feel my complete inadequacy, but I was tremendously
upheld in it all". The uncertainties of wartime, which helped encourage such
evangelism, were emphasised that month when one of the Fleet Air Arm's
most experienced pilots was killed in an accident, night flying from nearby
Kilindini. Commander T.P. Coode, a good friend of David's, had become
something of a legendary figure after bravely leading his squadron from the
*Ark Royal* in the successful attack on the giant battleship *Bismarck*.

David's return to England began in an oddly circuitous fashion, when
he was asked to fly a VIP (name unknown) from Nairobi to Khartoum, a
taxing 4-day enterprise in a Swordfish with stops at Kisumu, Soroti, Juba,
Malakal and Kosti. After waiting a week for his VIP in the Sudan, David
then took him on another 4-day flight, this time to the RAF station of
Fayid, 100 miles north-east of Cairo, via romantic-sounding bases like Wadi
Haifar, Aswan, Luxor and Heliopolis. So secret was the mission that David
was unable to mention it to his parents, but it probably related in some
way to the North African campaign, then at a most critical situation. The
Second Battle of Alamein had just been fought, ensuring that Rommel
would not capture Egypt, and the famous German tank commander was in
retreat, making his careful way towards Tunisia. David, however, this mission
over, flew on to a new station, Dakheila, outside Alexandria, where for a
week he trained some young pilots in the tired and soon-to-be-withdrawn
Blackburn Roc fighters. Shortly after crashing one of them, when a tyre
burst on landing, he learned, to his great joy, that there would soon be
transport to take him back, in stages, to England.

While awaiting the next leg home, he had the further joy of meeting
up with his elder sister Mildred who had been working in Cairo for seven
years as a teacher at the English Mission College. Together they visited
many of the most important archaeological sites, climbing the pyramids
and seeing the tombs of Tutankhamen and Ramases at Luxor. Mildred's
bold chauffeuring, however, was possibly the greatest excitement, as David
explained to their parents:

Have I described the business of flashing through Cairo by night with Mildred driving? It's one long miracle. Occasionally she explains, 'One's not *supposed* to overtake on the right, but if they *will* stay in the centre . . .' or 'This is *supposed* to be a one-way street, but if I'm quick I think I'll be all right.'

David and his sister Mildred, Cairo, February 1943

Mildred and the car with which she impressed David in Cairo

Less amusing for him were the obvious signs of degradation, greed and destitution so prevalent in British Egypt. He wrote in his diary:

This country is the most squalid I've been to. It really is a strain. Every moment someone is trying to sell you something - from a shoeshine to a haircut. They stand in doorways announcing everything from "a nice meal, sir" to "a good bed, sir". And if they're not trying to sell you something, they are trying to steal it. I am inclined to think the latter is the more honest! The waiters never make out a correct bill. And when you've pointed that out, they bring the wrong change. Even the hens lay small eggs.

In the Cairo streets David saw evidence of the worst that European colonisation could do to native integrity, and he contrasted the corrupt Egyptians with the unspoilt Africans elsewhere. He was unable to accept the traditional view of civilising European influences struggling with natural African weaknesses. To David, the fault lay entirely with the Europeans in their treatment of the Africans, and he was saddened by how readily and widely the Africans were criticised.

Eventually, in late February 1943, he took a 5-day flight from Egypt to Nigeria by BOAC flying-boat. En route he observed:

Although this has been the first day of my trip flying back to the UK I have felt very sad and depressed. I suppose it's chiefly my parting from Mildred that's still hurting, but I think also my impending departure from Africa. Not that I'm sorry to be leaving. Far from it, I'm afraid. But that's just it. I am afraid, afraid that now all the experiences and impressions I ought to remember will pass right from me, afraid that those that do remain available for recall from my subconscious will pop up disguised in the white raiment of wishful memory or the black robes of disappointment. Oh God, may I see and remember reality only, however hard and ugly it may be; and give me a true memory for all things beautiful, for all traces of man in Thine Own Image.

While at Lagos, he noted:

It was an interesting trip across the centre of Africa. We crossed hundreds of miles of desert, hundreds of miles of forest, hundreds of miles of swamps. The most isolated native villages here and there and a comparatively few European communities. At most of the latter we landed for refuelling. They looked grand from the air and even from the ground one often got the impression of enterprise and cleanliness, especially in the Belgian Congo where - superficially anyway - the effect was very good.

A visit to the Stanley Falls was marred by mass begging; that to Stanleyville (Kisangani) on the Congo, improved by the reception of a Ladies' committee which organised a visit to a swimming pool. At Leopoldville (Kinshasa) he bought his one and only souvenir - an ivory napkin ring. ("I only got it because he was such a charming old man to bargain with.")

David was not meant to stay long at Lagos, where he had stopped to change planes, but illness kept him there 3 weeks.

I was in the town when I was taken with sudden and excruciating pain in my shoulder and chest. The pain spread to my stomach and I was taken to hospital in a semi-conscious state.

He was treated for shock and, despite the climate, warmed with blankets and hot-water bottles. The doctors were mystified by the illness and unable to put a name to it.

The time spent in Lagos Hospital reinforced David's dismay at the average European attitudes towards the Africans, the European nursing sisters for ever criticising the so-called unreliability and cheek of the orderlies, whom David found uniformly engaging and helpful. He found it mirrored the European attitude to African clerks, traders and taxi-drivers:

It seems that it's only the very exceptional European who has much time for the African. This may be an overstatement, but it is my impression from east, north and west. And if South Africans from the Union are representative, it is even truer there. The general cry seems to blame education. Perhaps there is something in this, perhaps education for a few has been too fast, too European and, in consequence, insufficiently thorough. But how puzzling to the African must be the white man's inconsistencies. If a white man takes a black man's woman, nothing happens. But if a black man takes a white man's woman - imprisonment, flogging, even death. Is this the white man's justice? I am sure the faults we complain of in the African are really to a large extent our own fault. Not only faulty education, but faulty treatment by the very people who complain. Too little patience. No love. There are plenty of excuses for the Europeans - the climate alone is enough for me. In fact I am often filled with admiration for the efforts Europeans have made in spite of difficulties. But there it is . . . lack of love . . .

In another diary entry from Lagos, he wrote:

We must be patient with the African. Give him time. Give him care. Give him increasing responsibility. Give! Give! And expect no advantages in return. But from what I've seen of Africans, gratitude will be full and real.

He ended with a prayer:

Oh God, may our trusteeship be true and honest. Saviour of the world, I cannot bear that we should merit thy fearful condemnation - 'ye hypocrites!'

The period of observation in hospital over, David was briefly involved in testing various modified aircraft - the Albacore, Fulmar and Martlet - before eventually catching another flying-boat, a BOAC Boeing Clipper. On this final stage of his journey he noted:

I see a tremendous war proceeding. Enormous forces of evil threatening in a million separate fights to overwhelm an almost universal *desire* to do good. And this evil host seems to have the biggest of fifth-columns - a representative actually in almost every individual. And evidence has come to me this year which suggests once again that this has always been so: Egyptian carvings 3,000 years old show 'holy' monkeys in combat with 'evil' servants. The three questions of the Greek philosophers: Where do I come from? Where am I going? Why is there evil in my heart *which I don't want* but which I cannot control? Then Huxley: 'I protest that if some great power would agree to make me always think what is true and do what is right . . . I should instantly close with the offer.'

David's flying-boat eventually touched down in Poole harbour, Dorset, on 28 April 1943. As he reached England, well over a year after he had set out on an illuminating odyssey embracing Sri Lanka, Madagascar and much of Africa, he prayed that what was right and true would be the guiding principle in the future development of these countries and that the love of God would fill all hearts, particularly those currently downtrodden and unappreciated.

Africa is surely waking fast from an age-long sleep. Please God, may the growth of its worldly knowledge be accompanied by a real growth in the knowledge of Thee.

# 13

## JOS ON GIBRALTAR

In the middle of April 1943, just two weeks before David reached England, Jos had sailed from Gourock on the *Dunnottar Castle*, a liner-turned-troopship, steaming off to Gibraltar in a large convoy. The Rock, of course, had strong associations with the *Ark Royal*, and, soon after arriving there, Jos was telling his family:

It is interesting to think of David having been here for quite a time. His ship was very popular in the port and they still speak with respect for her. David, incidentally, has written to say, 'I regard you as taking over my foreign mission portfolio'!

Since the outbreak of war Gibraltar had been turned into a fortress, its women and children evacuated, its racecourse converted into an ad hoc airfield. It was feared that Hitler, to counter the Allied advance in North Africa, might well be contemplating taking over Spain and capturing Gibraltar. 3 and 9 Commandos had already done a spell on garrison duty there, and now it was 2 Commando's turn. It was certainly better than staying in Scotland, but, after so much training, the four-month posting was another frustration, particularly amid all the talk of a possible Second Front.

Jos's first letters home made it sound like a holiday:

I had the most glorious afternoon. We sunbathed and bathed alternately from 2:30 to 4:00. And in many ways it was exactly like Seaford in August (with just a little more sand)! Then (sorry, but I must tell the truth) back to tea and two oranges and two bananas. I only wish I could send you some home in this letter. They are of course profiteered, and oranges cost 3d or 4d and bananas 4d each. Strawberries are being sold at 3/-a pound . . .

Four days later he and his Troop commander Dickie Hooper toured Gibraltar on bicycles, assessing both the training and recreational possibilities.

The most obvious physical activity was digging:

You may have heard of the tunnelling that has been going on here. It certainly is amazing the old rock hasn't fallen in. It provides quite enough exercise in an otherwise very restricted area . . .

Soon 2 Commando were dutifully digging, day after day, to provide more soil for the extension of the very limited airfield. Training also involved a great deal of rock climbing and a single but ever-recurring assault exercise, 'Operation Seaweed', which involved going out to sea in two obsolete landing-craft and making an attack up a 'machine-gun-swept' beach against an imaginary power station. Jos's 6 Troop repeated 'Operation Seaweed' on seven occasions in one particularly repetitive week, sometimes for the benefit of visiting VIPs, the most important of whom was Winston Churchill.

The Navy put on a very spectacular show for the Prime Minister in this very happy break from the usual routine:

Every blunderbuss of every calibre on the Fortress hurled high explosive into the sky for 3 minutes, while Winston himself sat on the highest crag, witnessing the proceedings and smoking a monster cigar with the greatest satisfaction.

Occasionally, other celebrities came visiting:

This afternoon we had a glorious bathe, though got cuts and bruises from being biffed about on the rocks and shingle by the waves. We had the privilege of bathing next to Vivien Leigh, Beatrice Lillie and Leslie Henson who are here with an ENSA party!

A friendly atmosphere prevailed between the different ranks. Jos wrote of his 23rd birthday:

Officers of 2 Commando in Gibraltar. Jos is far right, back row. Frank Mason, far left back row. The central five seated are (l.-r.): Richard Broome, the Duke of Wellington, Churchill, Blissett and Hooper

On Thursday I took the Troop round for a bathe – they sang all the usual favourites, until we were on our way back and then we had in succession 'Poor Old Joe', 'Never Been 21 Before' and 'Happy Birthday to you'. Can you imagine it?! They're just a grand crowd of lads and I only hope I'm still with them when we first go into action . . .

While the men lived in sun-baked nissen huts, Jos and his fellow officers were much luckier, living in a small former nunnery which boasted a wireless – "They give us BBC programmes interspersed with Gibraltar Calling" – and a library. Early on, in their stay, Morny, the Duke of Wellington, slipped away quietly for a short while to visit family estates in nearby Spain where he was, apparently, a prince in his own right. Jos was finding him a delightfully modest, if slightly eccentric, companion, who enjoyed sharing reminiscences of schooldays at Stowe. Morny did his best to convince Jos that he could cure himself of the need to wear spectacles. He himself, he explained, had overcome poor eyesight by the Yogi system, which simply involved taking off one's spectacles, staring up at the sun through closed eyelids and gently relaxing. It was a wonderful cure, he assured Jos, but strangely, when Jos experimented, nothing seemed to happen . . .

The more he came to know Frank Mason, the more Jos liked the worldly-wise, ever-smiling former travelling salesman with a wife and child back in Cricklewood. As a keen horse-racing enthusiast and betting man, Mason was not going to let army regulations ruin the chance of making a few shillings on Derby Day:

Frank, aided and abetted by his pal John Jeffreys, set himself up as a bookie for the big race, erecting a large blackboard on the far corner of the square from where I happened to have been detailed to take Pay Parade for the whole Troop. As my pay queue steadily dwindled, so Frank's, over the way, steadily grew. Runners and riders were chalked up on the blackboard by the Troop Sergeant-Major; and Dickie Hooper's batman, the irrepressible Private Smith, harking back to his days as a barrow boy in the East End, shouted the odds.

Frank Mason's talents were wide-ranging. In another entrepreneurial plunge, he and John Jeffreys produced the first 'Green Berets' theatrical revue, which, taking its inspiration from the most popular variety artists of the day, the Crazy Gang, started a tradition of ad hoc commando entertainment. Another Mason-Jeffreys venture which Jos joined was a race to learn Spanish: "We've each bought a Hugo's Spanish Primer or a dictionary and have great fun trying out new words and phrases on one another." John Jeffreys quickly outpaced the others by dint of some quiet extra study. "John produced the Future Simple out of the bag this morning, whereas I am still struggling with the pronunciation . . ."

Frank Mason and Jos were regularly thrown together, and when Dickie Hooper, their Troop leader, decided to have one last attempt at getting a recalcitrant piece of shrapnel out of his leg, a legacy of the St Nazaire raid, they had a great time putting into practice training ideas which they "could never persuade Dickie to adopt". For a joint birthday celebration they braved a dance in a W.R.N.S. Mess, where Mason's extrovert antics delighted 'Bunny' (a Wren with slightly protruding teeth) more than 'Guardsman' (whose forbidding exterior may or may not have concealed a heart of gold).

Jos loved the lightheartedness of the Mason-Jeffreys approach to life, quickly assimilating it:

John Jeffreys has the *Faber Book of Comic Verse* – and we just find ourselves talking about slithy toads and cabbages & kings. We'll probably go into battle reciting 'If you bake me too brown, I must sugar my hair' or 'He looked again and saw it was a hippopotamus'.

Captain Pat Henderson, who had been at Stowe at the same time as Morny, became another important friend. He was as passionate a games player as Jos, and the two were soon helping a third school acquaintance who was in charge of all sport on the island. Jos's letters tell of makeshift sports days, hazardous cross-country races ("There were about 180 of us running in the boiling heat and I managed to scrape in 24th but poor John Jeffreys has broken a bone in his foot . . ."), belligerent basketball, disastrous squash ("Pat Henderson won his match but the rest of us lost!") and, of course, constant cricket, played on asphalt with an old matting wicket. The scrapes and bruises could not lessen the fun. "I got 2 wickets with about the only 2 balls which pitched," he reported. "Shades of Clarrie Grimmett!" And he exulted when one of the sergeants in his troop participated in a Rock record stand of 252 runs.

Another new friend was the impetuous young Alec Parsons. He had been serving with another unit on the Rock, where his madcap scrapes had already led to three official reprimands, the last one occasioned by an attempt to improve the men's rations by stealing a young pig in the dead of night from the Governor-General's farm. Alas, the pig squealed on him, and the Military Police closed in on Parsons at the moment when he and an accomplice were, with difficulty, manoeuvring the less than co-operative creature over a high wall.

Faced with the unexpected sight of the Military Police, Alec thought quickly, and, trading on a situation of divided loyalties, propelled the pig at the feet of the advancing coppers. The decision was tactically sound. Faced with a double problem – rapidly retreating miscreants, on the one hand, and an extremely slippery, noisy and ungracious pig, on the other – they selected the wrong option, and Alec and his friend quickly vanished into the shadows of the night . . .

Realising he might be better appreciated in boisterous 2 Commando, Parsons now put in an application for a transfer. His own unit released him most speedily.

Jos must have caused a certain amount of amusement to many of his high-spirited companions by the importance he attached to Sunday services. Right from the beginning he was writing home positively:

We had a very good Church Parade this morning. The dress was khaki shorts, shirts, no ties, sleeves rolled - very cool. The padre, a Welshman with grand descriptive powers, was the usual High Church sort - but he gave a very good sermon on the certainty of the Resurrection.

He also attended services at the Methodist Church:

I went to Communion with Dickie Hooper, and then for the 10.30 service to the Methodist Church - crammed full with Army, RAF and Navy types .... We had a splendid service run by some Plymouth Brethren on Sunday evening - it was good to hear the old hymns and use Sankey's 'Sacred Songs and Solos' again. The congregation was almost entirely military - the singing good - and the gospel talk first-class though of rather PB dictatorial style ...

On the Rock Jos first came into contact with one of the Army Scripture Readers, non-ordained but experienced Christians who were attached to a military unit in order to share their faith in an informal way. The ASR, who had won the Military Medal in the lst World War ("which makes a difference to the lads, who respect him"), was soon holding weekly evening services at the Gospel Hall at which Jos and one or two other officers also spoke to a group of about a dozen. After talking on Assurance (for which he used the illustration of Jesus walking on the water, from Matthew 14), Jos wrote home enthusiastically:

It is a grand way of keeping up to scratch and helps me no end to keep challenging myself. It is so easy to doubt and not to believe in the impossible - how well we all pray that we 'may know him'.

There was no-one in 2 Commando with the same strong evangelical background as his own, so it was a very broadening experience for him, and he learnt a great deal. He was able to give support to one member of Troop

5 who was having a particularly difficult time for having mentioned his Christian beliefs in the sergeants' mess. Things culminated one evening with a particularly ribald attack. 'Is this the *effing* Bible?' swore an antagonistic colleague, snatching it away. 'No,' replied the sergeant, as he quietly took it back. 'It's the *holy* Bible!' His calmness in the face of provocation had its effect. There was soon a different target for the ragging.

For Jos the months on Gibraltar were a further chance to extend his own reading. He told his parents: "The story of King David gives me great pleasure just at the moment and it's good to read the Psalms in conjunction with 2 Samuel . . ." Joshua had also been on his mind very much - "and particularly that 'he rose up early' on at least two occasions". He was much taken with Joshua's determination that 'this book of the law shall not depart out of my mouth' and the fact that it never did - "even when he waxed old and stricken in age". The last 2 chapters he found especially glorious: "I particularly love Chap. 23 v14: 'Not one thing hath failed of all the good things of which God spoke and ye know it in all your hearts and souls'."

Fortified by his faith, Jos coped rather better on Gibraltar than many of his fellow commandos who struggled with feelings of confinement and boredom. It was a well-known fact that only a few weeks on Gibraltar could produce 'Rock Happiness', an ironic term for deep discontent. And the officers caught it just as much as the men. Kipling's 'If' was popularly parodied in the old nunnery:

If you can fill the unforgiving minute
With things, if sane, you never would have done,
Yours is the rock, and everything that's in it,
And what is more, you'll be an ape, my son!

"You get fed up," Jos explained in one letter, "with seeing the same old wad of granite, the same faces etc., and a paralytic madness comes over you." Eventually the officers decided that this had better be faced, and an 'Off-The-Rock Society' was formed, which produced 'Exercise Nuts'. The Adjutant Harold Blissett, tongue in cheek, had posted Exercise Nuts in daily orders, and at 10 o'clock one night all the officers met up in the Mess in the old nunnery to carry out the instruction of "going mad for an hour". Jos gave his parents an edited version:

Some walked round just looking mad and behaving like apes – then everyone got on a chair and tried to shout everyone else down – a terrific hoot (I was terribly pleased to out-shout Harry Blissett!) Then the fun grew faster – first with a Scotch reel, led by John Jeffreys – then an all-in Rugger scrum – a boat race on some wooden forms and finally an auction sale of everything we could find.

There would also seem to have been a 'bullfight', and the 'boat race' somehow led to a chair disappearing out of a closed window, the glass on the floor giving the idea for the next game: 'Moving Round the Room Without Touching the Floor'. A spontaneous entertainment ensued called 'Finding a Subterranean Passage'. (2 Commando were of course by now real experts at digging . . .)

The volatile atmosphere was not calmed when, in mid-July, the Commando were told that their stay on the Rock was to continue:

To our utter dismay we have been left out of yet another 'show', and Sicily is being invaded without us. As one of my Troop said to me this morning, "Here am I sitting down as a hut orderly while the Second Front is opening up before my very eyes!" All we can do is to go on hoping that we won't be passed over next time . . . I'm afraid the Troops are lamenting the news of Sicily and our non-participation and using it as an excuse for getting drunk . . .

A few days later, as Jos sat down in the Mess to write a letter home outlining the latest initiatives of the Army Scripture Reader, he had to break off suddenly:

Sorry, I must stop! 'Exercise Crackers' is just beginning! Someone is trying to knock the piano to pieces with swing tunes, someone else is piping on the bosun's whistle and the Colonel has got his bagpipes out . . .

And after 'Exercise Crackers', came 'Exercise Potty' . . .

Eventually the long wait ended, and Lord Mountbatten himself arrived to tell 2 Commando in a rousing and much-cheered speech that there was "still work to be done in Sicily". The first attack had gone in a week earlier, with the British 8ᵗʰ Army under Montgomery landing at its south-east tip and the Americans under Patton in the west. The Germans were now being pushed back by this two-pronged attack towards the port of Messina, from where they were beginning to retreat to the Italian mainland. 2 Commando's task would be to cause aggravation to the German withdrawal.

On 18 July 1943, they boarded two converted cross-channel steamers, now being used as troopships, the *Prince Charles* and the *Princess Beatrix*. Before them was a thousand mile journey into the Mediterranean, with stops at Valletta, Tunis and Algiers. Jos had committed himself to becoming a commando. He had come through all the gruelling training. Now, at long last, he would be meeting his first test.

# 14
## JOS: SWEEPING UP IN SICILY

The long sea journey passed slowly, allowing Jos to make progress with *The Pilgrim's Progress*, one of the five books in his luggage. He was also taking into battle a German primer, the complete works of Shakespeare, his *Daily Light* and his Bible. This small-print Bible survives, together with a single sheet issued to all commandos, 'Prayers for use in Special Services Group'. The first of its two prayers was St Ignatius Loyola's, given a new title of 'An Act of Dedication' and chosen, no doubt, for its highly appropriate emphasis on giving without counting the cost and on fighting without heeding the wounds. The other prayer was "For my Home and Myself":

Almighty God, bless and guard my loved ones at home. Give me grace and strength to do my duty in what I believe to be a righteous cause; make me strong of heart and fearless in danger; and whether I live or die keep me in Thine almighty keeping, through Jesus Christ our Lord.

On the back of the sheet, placed by Jos in such a way that whenever he opened his Bible he was faced by it, was just a single verse from Joshua (1/9):

Be strong and of good courage; be not afraid, neither be thou dismayed: for the Lord thy God is with thee whithersoever thou goest.

They landed eventually, at night-time, at the port of Augusta on the south east side of Sicily, well inside territory conquered by the Allies, but in the middle of a German air-raid. An 8-mile night march followed, largely along cart tracks, until they reached a little village, Brucoli, surrounded by olive groves. On 22 July Jos wrote calmly:

6 Troop shortly before leaving Scotland: front row (l.-r.): Sgt. Heery, Serg.Maj. Bishop, Lt. Frank Mason, Capt. Richard Hooper, Jos, Sgt. Prescott, Sgt. Furse, Sgt. Smallbone

For obvious reasons I cannot say much in this letter - except to assure you that by and large this is an exceptionally peaceful island from what we see of it . . . To get here, we had what in peacetime would have been a really expensive Mediterranean cruise. Quite delightful.

They stayed under canvas at Brucoli for three full weeks, waiting and wondering. The mid-day heat that August was intense, flies and mosquitoes intolerable, facilities primitive and dysentary common. They soon began to loathe the place. Fortunately Colonel Jack Churchill kept them fully occupied, amusing them with a new device he had just invented for hurling arrows at unsuspecting sentries, and instilling in them his latest idea, soon known as the 'Mad Minute', an exactly timed 60 seconds, from the moment an assaulting party was in position, during which the covering fire party would give the enemy everything it had. Then, to the exact second, the covering fire ceased and the assault would go in.

Jos filled in off-duty hours with quiet reading. Having finished *The Pilgrim's Progress*, he was now well through the other half of Bunyan's book, *The Holy War*, an allegory on the progress of the Christian soul. Occasionally Jos wandered over to the one wireless in camp, to try to verify the news.

It is funny to have to wait for news from London about what is actually happening not so far away from here. The general hope is that the Italians won't give up just yet, and that we can have a crack at them. But it looks as if there are barely two people with the same ideas in Italy just now . . .

The daytime heat was stifling. They slept at night under small almond trees and the stars, and washed in the local streams night and morning. Rumour had it that Catania had now been captured and the Germans were retreating to Messina, intending to evacuate the whole island. Each extra day of waiting at Brucoli was bringing false alarms: "We pack, unpack, pack, embark, disembark, unpack, pack ad infinitum!"

Eventually, on 14 August, 2 Commando finally left for combat, and, after marching the 8 miles back to Augusta, embarked on the *Prince Charles*, where Major General Sir Oliver Lees (one of Montgomery's key commanders) gave them a stirring pep talk. The 8th Army, in trying to clear the Germans right out of the island, had been held up at Taormina by a series of roadblocks along the only coastal road, about sixteen miles from Messina. 2 Commando were to be landed eight miles inside enemy lines at a little fishing village, Scaletta, halfway between Taormina and Messina.

Aerial reconnaissance suggested that the beach on which they were to land was wire-protected, with machine-guns posts at each end. Beyond lay a road and, running parallel, a railway line. 2 Commando's mission was to establish a bridgehead and "try to cut off as much of the Jerry armour between Taormina and Messina as possible". 6 Troop was part of the initial assault team, whose first objective would be a gun battery, lying behind the village, somewhere to the right. Half of the unit, meanwhile, would land to the north of the bay's headland and provide the 'Mad Minute'. That, at least, was the theory . . .

2 Commando readied themselves on the troopship at 3 o'clock in the morning for the impending action:

The night was intensely still and there was a clear moon. Silently we moved out of the Mess decks, which had only been lit with dim red lights, and where it had been hard to see. Bren gun magazines were now being filled, grenades primed, and the awkward Bangalore torpedoes (metal tubes containing explosives and a firing mechanism, used to blow up wire entanglements) prepared, while final orders were being given, aerial photographs examined and faces blackened.

Three miles offshore the parent ship unloaded the commandos, transferring them into small landing craft, which hung on davits a few feet below deck level. Each man had equipment and ammunition to last forty-eight hours. As Jos and his men were getting into their craft a vivid red flash from a distant explosion lit up the night sky.

Each craft was lowered into the sea . . . The engines were soon running and we swung away from the parent ship. All heads had to be kept below the gunwale and we could only see the moon and stars above us. The agony now began. The sea got up and as we hit each wave a splash of water fell over us, soaking everything. It got worse as the tiny craft rolled, and some men were sick. It took an hour and half to reach the shore, but seemed an age. The one satisfaction was that the first fear had gone and there was only a great desire to get out.

Jos sat on the front slat with Sergeant Heery, a Bangalore torpedo across their knees, regularly checking in his pocket for the matches with which he would light the fuse.

Peering over the bows I could see the outline of the coast. The hills were extraordinarily clear, and soon it became possible to distinguish beaches and headlands. But now the naval lieutenant in charge of the navigation seemed to have second thoughts about our direction, and the leading craft slowed down, and we all followed suit. I felt sure we were going in the right direction, but apparently the navigating officer, unable to spot a large white house which had shown up clearly in the photographs, turned northwards.

They were to learn in due course that this was indeed an error of judgement:

Running parallel along the coast was an eerie experience. I felt that a thousand and one eyes were watching the craft, and waiting to see what we would do before unleashing everything on us. For a mile or so we moved on, then the Mad Minute group which were to land a little to the north of us moved away, and our seven craft turned in towards the beach, moving from line ahead to line abreast. About 400 yards out, the engines were put to full speed ahead. Silence now didn't matter, as surprise had been lost. With heart thumping and praying that I wouldn't make a fool of myself, I leant forward, bracing myself for the shock of hitting the beach.

Had they been assaulting a heavily defended beach, the odds would have very much favoured Jos's first moments of active service being his last. But, mercifully, they were not:

Our craft came to a stop with a crunch against the pebbles. For an eternity the chains allowed the front to drop forward, while the bullet-proof sides offered their last protection. Before it was flat, Heery and I were rushing out. Crashing out over the yielding shingle, we ran for the wire. But it wasn't there. And the silence remained unearthly . . .

Rushing on, Jos and his troop found themselves at a low embankment. Jos peered over the top. It was the railway. No sign, as yet, of the Catania-Messina road, wending its way round the foothills of Mount Etna. No sign, as yet, of any Germans. Jos's section of 6 Troop was joined by Frank Mason's together with the Troop Leader Dickie Hooper. It was clear that they been put down on the wrong beach, and that the evacuation was further advanced than the Allied planners had realised. A day or so earlier they would have found this part of the coast swarming with Germans. It was hard to tell the extent of the enemy's hold of this area, but they were certainly on the move.

Hooper at once made the decision to follow the railway line left, in the direction of what was clearly the village of Scaletta. They had only just started, when they were momentarily startled by a huge explosion way off to their left, where 2 Troop had not only come across the road but also a German lorry loaded with explosives on its way towards Messina. 100,000 Germans and Italians would eventually make the crossing from Messina to mainland Italy and temporary safety. But not this lorry. The huge noise heard was the lorry exploding into flames when hit by the commandos in a costly exchange of fire. One of the problems in this kind of disorganised, desultory street fighting was the danger of firing on friend rather than foe. The importance of loud, clear passwords was essential. But establishing friendly or hostile credentials could also cost valuable seconds, and, in the act of making such a password challenge, John Jeffreys had been shot and killed.

6 Troop, meanwhile, were still trying to manoeuvre their way through the outskirts of the village. The main road had now been identified, and they decided to make use of a narrow archway which led under the railway line towards it. Going through this low culvert, however, had potential dangers and Jos sent his Sergeant and Corporal to a nearby garden to cover their approach. As he led a cautious foray forwards, a machine-gun opened up from the archway. "All at once we were in the thick of it." They scattered.

The gun fired twice again. I was forced into a doorway. I battered at the woodwork, but was unable to make the slightest impression. There was no handle and no lock . . .

Jos fired his automatic at the unseen assailants. Back came a significant response.

I felt a sharp biff in the back, but, realising that nothing hurt, thought no more about it. It was only afterwards, when I took off my pack that I noticed two small holes in it. On top was a bren gun magazine, at an angle, which now had a large dent in it. The round inside the magazine was bent. I had had a rather remarkable escape. The jagged piece of metal would, in normal circumstances, have passed through the pack and cut a nasty hole in the back of my neck. Instead, it had ricocheted off . . .

Dickie Hooper, meanwhile, had sprinted off with Frank Mason and Sergeant Prescott, and eliminated the machine gun which was causing the problems, though not before Sergeant Heery and a corporal from Jos's section had been caught in the fire, one killed outright, the other wounded. Sergeant Prescott (the cricketer who had scored a century in that record first-wicket stand at Gibraltar) had been severely wounded in the attack on the machine-gun post and Dickie Hooper incapacitated, shot in the shoulder, though he refused to get his wound dressed and carried on leading his men for the whole morning. Regrouping as best they could, 6 Troop made their way to the village centre, high in the cliffs, Scaletta Superiore.

There they met with disorganised, piecemeal resistance from those Germans who had been taken by surprise while resting in the village en route to Messina. Everywhere there were signs of mass withdrawal, and at Scaletta Superiore they found some abandoned twenty-five pounder guns, mounted on the chassis of a Sherman tank. They quickly withdrew, however, as the area came under heavy mortar attack from unseen Germans in higher positions.

The big question now was whether to move south towards Taormina, or north towards Messina. After reconnoitring south down the shell-damaged road, they started towards Messina, but were held up for the afternoon and evening by continuous mortar fire. As night fell, 6 Troop occupied a small promontory on the flank, as other Troops moved through. While in this defensive position, Jos heard German being spoken - an eerie sensation in the middle of the night. It was coming, they discovered, from a mortar observation point, and its subsequent capture added to the number of prisoners 2 Commando had taken on that first, long day:

I was able to catch up again on my German by practising it on a few prisoners we nabbed. It is certainly much better than my Italian - I just can't start to cope with that language, and I have to wait till I meet one of the many Sicilians who have been to the USA ... It was so strange talking to someone on the other side - rather like the sort of restraint at a rugger tea or a cricket interval! There was so much you could talk about and so little you did.

Before dawn they were on the move again, making for Messina, and now under the overall command of General Currie's 4th Armoured Brigade. The political situation in south Italy was highly volatile - Mussolini was in hiding, having been ousted by the Italians themselves and replaced by

Marshal Badoglio - and Jos witnessed a considerable change of heart from the dazed local population:

Painfully slowly, in the face of the menace of minefields, we wended our way those eight miles. As we got closer and closer to the town, around 10 in the morning, the locals began to come out. Cautiously at first, but then with ever increasing enthusiasm. At first they clapped and blew kisses or threw flowers, later fruit of all sorts and paper streamers, in their joy at getting rid of the Germans. The people of Messina were making a monster fiesta out of it all.

It showed great spirit. Messina itself, both town and port, had been very badly bombed. And now Nazi coastal guns on the other side of the straits, at Reggio, were opening up on it.

Transport was commandeered later that afternoon, when, on the order to evacuate, 2 Commando returned all the way back to Catania, some distance beyond their landing-place, Scaletta. There in due course they held a memorial service and buried their dead. Though their losses were dwarfed by the scale of the immense sacrifice needed to liberate Sicily - 5,000 Allied soldiers losing their lives - they were no less bitter for that. Jos never forgot the effect John Jeffreys' death had on his fellow section-leader:

Frank Mason was inconsolable at the news. 'Frankie and Johnnie' had been their theme song, and they had been inseparable. John, the dashing cavalier, Frank, the quick-witted fighter, each typifying one aspect of the complete Commando soldier. Frank took the separation very hard and he was never quite the same person again. He lost his capacity for jollity.

Later, in a Sicilian orange grove, they held a service of thanksgiving for the fall of Messina. Jos gave thanks, too, for the bren gun magazine at the top of his pack, without which his endeavours, like those of poor John Jeffreys, would have come to a sudden end in the foothills of Mount Etna. As it was, he was merely put on the list of 'very slightly wounded' when it was discovered he had "the minutest portion of shrapnel" in his leg.

As August ended, 2 Commando were uncomfortably encamped in lemon groves, with dust and flies everywhere, an unreal sense of business-as-usual permeating the atmosphere. In his letters home, Jos, like David before him, tried hard to minimise the dangers and sound as light-hearted as possible:

Just back from driving on these awful Sicilian roads. The 8th Army tell us they were many times worse in North Africa - but that's rather hard to believe. I was driving a 15 cwt Dodge! All right, you can guess what a noise came from that gearbox and you'd be dead right.

Descriptions of the local area made for useful digressions, and helped his family imagine something of his current existence:

—The Sicilians are a nation of barbers, and those are some of the very few shops that are open in the towns. But they are just about as good as the Spaniards and love to pour on the unguents and powders . . . To encourage the local populace to get on their feet again, most of the towns are made out of bounds to troops, except on special passes. But the restaurants and lemonade booths are pretty poor so it is not much of a disadvantage . . .

—The locals are coming back from their places of hiding into the towns so we have to live out in the open under the stars and lemon branches . . . Sea bathing is a relief but it is really too warm and is too salty to get any of the dirt off at all . . .

—We went into the local town this morning and were able to buy ice creams - I pegged it and ate 4 to Frankie's 2!! But there wasn't much else worth buying except the odd pears (not quite ripe).

—We live on rumours as usual. It's a good job there are no 5th Columnists about as they would be sending back to Lord Haw Haw exactly what we and the rest of the world are not going to do or have not done.

Writing gentle letters home was therapeutic after the painful ones he was now having to write to the families of the killed and wounded. Jos particularly struggled to find the right words for John Jeffreys' mother, just as he did a few days later, when he met John Jeffreys' brother, who was also serving in Sicily. ("I shall never forget having to tell him about John's death. I didn't get very far because I found it impossible to go on . . .")

For Jos, as for David, the tragic loss of friends amid the horrors of war did not undermine confidence in the existence of a God of love, but, rather, exemplified the forces of evil long at work in the world. As he mourned in

Catania, moreover, Jos found himself pondering on Jesus's words (in Mark chapter 5) to the former outcast, Legion: "Go home to thy friends and tell them how great things the Lord hath done for thee." And he felt more strongly than ever a need to overcome natural diffidence and, despite all the pressures of the time, to try to interest those around him in the faith for which he himself was so very grateful.

# 15

# DAVID: DISCUSSIONS AT THE ADMIRALTY

David was by now up on the east coast of Scotland, beginning a new phase of his Fleet Air Arm service. His leave home, on his return from Africa, had been a particularly productive one, involving several trips to the Admiralty in London to discuss his immediate future. David had become more and more interested in the Fleet Air Arm's Service Trials Unit (778 Squadron), which since the start of the war had tested new aircraft, armament and equipment and evaluated and recommended fresh tactics. Its work, he felt, had not always been as effective as it might have been, by being almost totally theoretical. So much more might be achieved, he believed, and so many lives saved, if the Service Trials Unit became a practical testing body, operating from its own aircraft carrier. The Admiralty not only liked the idea but decided that David, as a newly-promoted Lieutenant-Commander, should create his own unit, 778's 'B Flight', a team of pilots and back-up crew who would put to practical test at sea the latest ideas thought up by the boffins of the Service Trials Unit.

Despite all this, David had found his return to England curiously unsettling, his experiences in Ceylon, East Africa and Madagascar seeming strangely surreal from the perspective of Reigate and the placid Surrey countryside in late springtime. And it was hard to equate the chaotic, almost shambolic nature of war, as he had experienced it, with the measured tones of its description on the radio. And, of course, the radio rarely told all that was actually happening. The atrocities of war took time to reveal themselves in all their full horror. While he was on leave, for example, there had been no news of the ruthless suppression of the latest Jewish uprising in the Warsaw ghettos, let alone the quarter of a million ghetto dwellers who had subsequently disappeared in the Treblinka extermination camp.

The war was real enough, of course, in London, which in the aftermath of the Battle of Britain was now under a new form of aerial attack-from German fighter planes converted to tip-and-run bombers. And on this particular leave David found himself quite often in London, not just to visit the Admiralty, but also to see Jos's sister, Joanna, who, on leaving school, had started out as a trainee nurse at the Middlesex Hospital.

In early May 1943 David was back on Navy business, piloting an Albacore from London to Arbroath (a large Fleet Air Arm training establishment) to begin work on the selection of B Flight's personnel and answer queries about the *Pretoria Castle*, a Union Castle ocean liner currently in a Glasgow shipyard undergoing conversion as a carrier. Before him was an immense challenge, the vindication of the Admiralty's decision to enlarge the Service Trials Unit and implement his own very expensive ideas. So much more would be required of him in this newly created job than just his flying skills. Never before had he shouldered such a responsibility. He could not have coped with the prospect, he knew, without the assurance of his faith. One sentence from the psalms, in particular, he had appropriated for all his wartime flying, and no doubt it was with him as he flew up to Arbroath and all the challenges of a new life as a test pilot in charge of a trials unit: "If I rise on the wings of the dawn, if I settle on the far side of the sea, even there your hand will guide me, your right hand will hold me fast."

# 16
## JOS AT SALERNO (I)

Jos and 2 Commando left the dusty, malaria-ridden orange groves around Catania at the end of August 1943 for a new base across the island, just outside Palermo. It was not the easiest of journeys:

It was fantastic to see how the road wound up and down the hills. It never kept to the valleys – and every town or village was placed on the top of the highest hill available. The roads were appallingly bad–particularly on the back of a lorry crowded with equipment and cooking utensils. Luckily we managed to put up at a farmhouse for the night and bought some eggs off the owner . . .

Camping in fields outside the heavily-bombed Palermo (reputedly the world's most conquered city), they discovered they were part of a newly-formed Special Services Brigade (which also included Royal Marine 41 Commando and the American Rangers), attached to the American section of the 5$^{th}$ Army. This produced immediate advantages – "for the first time since coming abroad there were no complaints about the food" – but they were tantalised by the deliberately vague briefings they were given about their next commitment:

Maps were issued with all the names carefully cut out, and the verbal orders had no mention of our destination. The general objectives were (i) to establish a firm beachhead and reconnoitre 4 towns and (ii) to advance northwest, preparatory to an attack on a huge port.

2 Commando's own specific mission was for the moment was equally vague: they would (i) assault a beach and (ii) reconnoitre a town. Colonel Jack

Churchill and his second-in-command, Major Tom Lawrie, were said to be the only ones who knew the top-secret details. But an American GI lorry driver at the camp was offering anyone who cared to listen what turned out to be an alarmingly accurate forecast of action centred around Salerno, on the south-west coast of Italy.

It would later transpire that the British 8th Army under Montgomery had already made landings at the toe and heel of Italy, at Reggio and Tarento, and now the 5th Army, the first ever combination of British and American troops (100,000 British and 75,000 American) was to make a four-pronged assault (codename Operation Avalanche) not just at Salerno but across a huge, 40-mile front. In the 1930s Salerno had been a prosperous resort with its own Lido and an elegant promenade lined with palm trees, but by the summer of 1943 even the locals had largely evacuated the city and left it to the military, those remaining behind hiding in cellars and tunnels during the two months of Allied aerial bombing which preceded the attempted landings. Operation Avalanche was aptly named, for it was to be the biggest amphibious invasion yet seen in history. As the early briefings had indicated, the landings were to be followed by a "northwest advance" towards the "huge port" of Naples, which was planned to fall into Allied hands only five days into the invasion.

That, at least, was the theory. The event was to prove very different, the vast beachhead itself only finally being secured after three weeks of intense and bloody fighting, for the place chosen for the landings, ringed as it was by sizeable mountains, presented serious problems for an invading army and considerable help to the area's defence. This was now almost entirely German - 5 elite Panzer divisions of Hitler's Wehrmacht - since, just before the operation began, Marshal Bagoglio had negotiated an armistice between Italy and the Allies. This betrayal, in German eyes, made the defence of Salerno all the more ferocious, the 21-day battle becoming one of the most hard-fought turning-points of the war, for after the initial landings had been relatively successful, the Germans threw massive reserves into a major counter-attack and this so nearly succeeded that General Mark Clark, supreme commander of the 5th Army, at one stage seriously contemplated withdrawal from Italy. If 2 Commando had missed out on most of the fighting in Sicily, they had certainly not done so this time.

They left for Salerno on 8 September 1943 on board another converted cross-channel ferry, the *Prince Albert*, and in due course became part of an armada of 500 ships.

The sea passage was mostly in daylight. Gradually the convoys from Malta and North Africa, which together made up the new Allied 5th Army, joined our Palermo convoy. At about 1300 hours the island of Capri was sighted. Everyone was a bit staggered to be so close to the mainland so soon. Yet, apart from one short aerial bombardment at 2100 hours, the journey was itself uneventful.

Soon the 5th Army, still out of range of the coastal guns, was spreading itself out along the assault area. Because the Special Service Brigade was specifically trained to operate in difficult conditions, the three units of Commandos were positioned on the extreme left, their job to secure the mountainous west flank of the whole operation, the wild country above and beyond Vietri-sul-Mare, which dominates and controls the Molina Pass below, through which the whole army would need to travel in the subsequent push north, via Vesuvius, to Naples.

With the American Rangers on their left (and landing at Maiori), 2 Commando (together with Royal Marine 41 Commando) were to land at Vietri, in peacetime a popular tourist resort, for it lies at one end of the spectacularly scenic southern side of the Sorrento peninsula (stretching past Amalfi to Positano), much admired for its quaint old-fashioned little towns with pastel-shaded houses and winding cobbled streets, clinging to towering cliffs which rise almost sheer from pretty little beaches. 2 Commando's immediate objective was to knock out the German coastal defence battery on top of the cliffs at Vietri; to root out any enemy in the mountainous area behind it; to cause as many problems as possible on the western outskirts of Salerno; and, with the Rangers and Royal Marines, to ensure the security of the all-important Molina Pass, which ran between two mountains (later known as Dragonea and Monument Hills).

The invasion enjoyed no element of surprise, the Germans having plenty of time to blow up the harbour and other useful coastal facilities which invading forces might appropriate. 2 Commando's adjutant (Harold Blissett) later wrote that, as they waited offshore, "towards midnight great fires could be seen on the eastern beaches and explosions could be heard. There was a blazing ship on the waterline some distance away which cast a dull glow over the surface of the sea." The first phase of the assault began, simultaneously on all fronts, at 2.30 in the morning. For 2 Commando, this consisted of 1-3 Troops, who transferred from the *Prince Albert* to five landing craft, and were commanded by 'Mad Jack', armed with his lightweight Beretta and favourite claymore, his batman dutifully carrying, in case of immediate need, his crossbow, arrows and bagpipes. A minesweeper led them in, while the destroyer *Blackmore* pounded away at what were thought to be the most likely enemy gun battery positions.

Jos and 4-6 Troops awaited anxiously for two hours the return of the landing craft:

The night seemed extraordinarily quiet . . . No news came back to the *Prince Albert*. Did it mean there was no opposition or had all the wirelesses already been knocked out? We stood on deck, straining our eyes into the darkness. At last, at about 0430 hours, the noise of our landing craft could be heard. As soon as they came within hailing distance, there were frantic queries across the water. 'It's a doddle,' came the answer.

A doddle, however, it wasn't, as they very soon found out. They were not to know, but the 15th Panzer Division stood between them and the road to Naples.

The sea was calm and the silence so complete that the men in my craft even asked me if they could smoke. As we approached the little beach at Marina, a thousand metres away from Vietri-sul-mare, there was a big splash in the water in front of us. 'Our perishing destroyers dropping short', said someone. But another in the sea behind us made us realise that we really were the target. The coxswain went to full speed, as German mortar bombs began to land in the sea all around. We went into the beach very hard.

As Jos and his comrades raced across it, they were mortared by defenders in the hills and sprayed with episodic machine-gun fire. The boats pulled away at once, the coxswains believing, wrongly, that the beach was still in enemy hands, and so took with them all the stores and reserve ammunition they should have unloaded. Jos and his companions, having sprinted through the mayhem on the beach, found some protection from the tall buildings on either side of the steep, cobble-stoned street leading up to the main road, which, via an exposed viaduct, brought them to Vietri itself, high above sea level. At the top of the town Jos, Frank Mason and 6 Troop found 'Mad Jack' ensconced in what had once been a school before its conversion into a Nazi headquarters building. There they learned that 1-3 Troops had experienced comparatively little trouble in establishing themselves in the town, the Germans seemingly having opted to take up defensive positions in the mountains behind. The gun battery, facing out to sea from the top of the cliffs, had been hastily dismantled and smashed, though not all the Germans had made good their departure from Vietri and several had already been captured.

The various Troops of 2 Commando were soon well scattered, actively pursuing the objectives of silencing random snipers and machine-guns posts and clearing any Germans out of the area between Vietri and the western edge of Salerno. Troop 6 was given the job of holding the town. A third landing phase had brought in anti-tank gun crews and a mortar company, and Jos's section was now temporarily augmented by two six-pounder guns. Choosing as his temporary section base a house reported to be empty, Jos burst in to discover a fat Italian admiral in the process of changing into civilian clothes. Like all Italians, the Admiral had been left in a difficult position by Marshal Badoglio's armistice. Some had responded to the humiliation by proudly fighting on, sometimes for the Axis, but also, in some cases, for the Allies. Others, like the Admiral (who had been in charge of the harbour before its demolition) preferred to slip back anonymously into civilian life. He greeted Jos effusively, like a lost friend, and immediately pressed upon him a bar of medals as a token of his deep esteem.

By the afternoon Jos had established his anti-tank guns on a high terrace between Vietri and Salerno, his machine-guns protecting any approach from the road immediately below (today's Strada Statale 18). He himself, meanwhile, was in a more forward position with his riflemen. When a tank from Salerno suddenly appeared 900 yards away, his 6-pounders immediately went into action, scoring two direct hits, but a second German Tiger appeared and quickly retaliated.

The shots exploded behind me. Moving back to see what damage had been done, I found that one of the shots had landed in a tree directly above the bren gun position and had knocked out most of the crew. Barnes, Basire and Williams had all been wounded. Williams had caught it in the throat, but, cheerful, irresponsible Cockney that he was, he wrote later to one of his buddies from his hospital bed, "I now talk like Nat Gonella sings". Further back, Charles Lea, our young Intelligence Officer who had already won the George Medal, was killed outright ...

Meanwhile Pat Henderson, the friend with whom he had organised so many sporting events in Gibraltar, had led 1 Troop down to the level of the road and bravely persisted in a close-range, if unequal, fight with the tank. For a time they were sprayed by masonry and shrapnel from shells exploding against the house directly behind them. Then Henderson moved forward alone with a clumsy, heavy and far-from-effective anti-tank gun with which, eventually, he landed a successful shot on the turret, causing the tank's smoky withdrawal back towards Salerno. He was later awarded the Military Cross.

There was heavy German mortaring of Vietri throughout the day. Miraculously, the church of San Giovanni, a lovely building with a pretty yellow and blue majolica-tiled dome and white bell tower, survived intact. In the late afternoon, when 4 Troop was briefly resting in the town, its commanding officer Captain Tom Gordon Hemming came across a priest and persuaded him (by the use of some schoolboy Latin) to hold a service there and then. News quickly spread. The church filled up, shell-shocked locals mingling with 4 Troop, and there was a marvellous moment of Anglo-Italian rapprochement as Tom Gordon Hemming accompanied the black-robed priest out of the sacristy as the short, ad hoc service began. Few of the commandos were Catholics, but sectarian niceties somehow didn't matter.

2 Commandos' long first day in Salerno seemed to have been successful. But by the next morning things were not nearly so promising. The main landings just east of Salerno had met with the fiercest of resistance. The

orders of Field Marshal Kesselring from the German high command had been unequivocal: "The invading army must be completely annihilated and thrown into the sea." There had not, as yet, been annihilation, but there had been extremely heavy losses. Military equipment, meant to facilitate the triumphant progress to Naples, lay like grotesque works of art abandoned on beaches littered with corpses.

And on the extreme west flank, too, there were problems. A German patrol had climbed Monument Hill, on the far side of the valley, from where they began shelling Vietri. 1-3 Troops, under cover from Arthur Brunswick's mortar group, made a speedy approach, killed some and captured the rest. But there was a worse problem on Dragonea Hill, up above Vietri, on the near side of the valley, where the Marines had come under heavy attack from German patrols; their headquarters had been hit and their Colonel seriously wounded. Vietri itself was now threatened. So 4, 5 and 6 Troops were ordered to their assistance. Jos later wrote:

Frank Mason gave me the news. The Germans had infiltrated through and might be anywhere on Dragonea Hill. There was one map and no other information. 6 Troop padded down the street of Vietri and met some bren carriers. 'Are you going up the hill?' 'Yes, why?' 'We're to take you there, that's why!' So we piled in. With the usual loud exhaust they moved off. Where the viaduct across the valley forked off from the main Cava (Molina Pass) road, the carriers stopped. 'It's a bit unhealthy here,' our driver said. 'We'll make a dash for it.' He accelerated forward with a shout of 'Keep Down!' and raced across. A shot rang out, but we were safe. None of the following carriers were hit, either, but the viaduct had several extra chips taken out of it. Round the corner, the carriers stopped again. 'From here on, you walk.'

Dragonea Hill took its name from a village of a few ramshackle, yellow-stuccoed houses, situated halfway up its slopes. It had been around this village that the Marines had met with a fierce counter-assault from German paratroopers, led by a young Austrian, Major Josef Fitz, commander of the 2nd Parachute Battalion of the highly-respected Hermann Göring Panzers, which had been hastily sent down from Rome. Fitz was already a veteran of campaigns in Poland and Russia, and a legendary figure among his men for the dramatic way he would urge them on from the turret of his tank, shouting furious *Sieg Heils* and brandishing his Luger.

Jos, Frank Mason and 6 Troop knew nothing of the presence of the Hermann Göring Panzers as they climbed up in the early evening through terraced fields of vines and olive groves. As they went higher, they passed recent battlegrounds where both British and German bodies still lay burning, relics of a barrage of phosphorus bombs. Eventually, around midnight, 4-6 Troops linked up with the Royal Marines, who were huddled in deathly silence in slit trenches on a hilltop, high up, miles seemingly from anywhere. 6 Troop dug in as best they could:

With our entrenching tools we all hacked at the thin layer of soil that covered the rock on that hill top. Frank Mason and I posted sentries and arranged to sleep alternately.

During the night the silence continued, apart from one shot, on their right, where 5 Troop's commander, Guy Whitfield, had killed a German officer who was trying to infiltrate their positions. The next morning, too, passed in eerie silence. Were the Germans biding their time? Perhaps they had withdrawn?

As the lack of any Nazi presence started to seem a reality, the commandos, who had mostly had no rest for 48 hours, were withdrawn from the line and replaced with infantry from the main army. However, with the Lincolns and King's Own Yorkshire Light Infantry barely in position, Major Fitz suddenly struck, charging forward with 600 men, driving the British infantrymen down the slopes with their Spandau machine-guns, re-capturing the bullet-pocked village of Dragonea and taking scores of prisoners. Caught in this onslaught, British troops staggered from their hillside dugouts in surrender.

As news of the crisis reached 2 Commando headquarters, the newly-returned 4-6 Troops were at once sent back up Dragonea Hill.

It was a steep climb on a stifling hot day . . . We could see right across the valley. Everything was deceptively still and attractive. In the far distance was White Cross Hill. 'Look!' said Frank Mason to me. 'The cross still stands.' There on the top of the hill, already much fought over, the battered Christian emblem still stood, despite every man-made effort to reduce it to nothing. Many times later I would remember that comment of Frank's, that message of hope in dark days.

The Germans were thought to have regrouped and dug themselves in on the hill. So 4–6 Troops climbed up, intent on finding defensible positions, covering the forward slopes. Innumerable stone walls made conventional army tactics of fire and movement unworkable. With Dickie Hooper wounded, Frank Mason was now in command of 6 Troop:

The terraces made Frank's job easier, because slit trenches could be dug at the end of each terrace and the whole length covered. The difficulty was the narrowness of each terrace and the considerable drop between them.

Positioned on the left of Richard Broome's 5 Troop and Tom Gordon Hemming's 4 Troop, with marine commandos on either side of them, they waited and waited. Though they were still unopposed as night fell, it soon became clear that there was now a considerable enemy force mustering. There were sounds of various forms of transport, of tank engines, even of German voices-paratroopers, as it turned out, and panzer-grenadiers and *nebelwerfer* crews (the *nebelwerfer* mixing poison gas with high explosive). It was impossible to sleep. Many quietly readied their weapons, again and again, for something to do.

In Section Two of 6 Troop, Jos and Sergeant Hill alternated on guard every two hours. As Hill had lost his watch, Jos lent him his own:

Half an hour later I was having a strange dream. Someone was knocking at the door and simply would not come in. At last, through the mists of sleep I realised that it was a continuous sound of thumping and banging. The whole front of the hill was being mortared. I looked around. Gunner Chick Burns, a quiet little Scot, in the slit trench beside me, was wide awake but motionless.

A violent concentration of German bombing lasted over half an hour. At Commando H.Q., just below the village of Dragonea, adjutant Harry Blissett found it "murderous". When it eventually stopped, Jos realised that it was too early for what he had taken to be early morning mist to be real. It was smoke coming from *nebelwerfers*. From out ahead came the rattle of machine guns, the rapid staccato of the German Spandaus. Then a single bren firing short bursts. The odd rifle shot and the odd shout. Finally, the noise of men coming through the trees towards them.

It was the scattered remnants of 5 Troop, who'd been attacked by a large force of German paratroopers and were now falling back. The Troop's leader, Richard Broome, had been killed. 3 brens were out of action. There was an urgent need to shorten the line. Jos had just passed this on to Frank Mason, when a German paratrooper materialised in front of him. In a rapid exchange of fire, Jos emptied his Browning automatic, and the German dived or fell behind a boulder. Jos waited for a sight of him, expecting him to fire round this cover, but he never did. Mason meanwhile had received his orders from H.Q. and shouted to Jos, "Get your section together. I'll cover you out. We've got to move - to get back to the walls, about 100 yards behind us."

Gunner Burns, in the trench beside Jos, was motionless. Jos poked him, but there was no response. He'd been shot through the forehead. Grabbing as much of Burns' ammunition as he could carry, Jos crept up to Private Davies' slit trench.

There was nothing to see. The sides had caved in. I scratched away at the earth. Underneath were the charred remains of poor old Taffy, an ex-policeman who'd trained with me at Achnacarry, a magnificent person, good solid worth.

Gathering his riflemen and bren gunners, Jos moved swiftly back to the wall. It was the preface to a relentless morning of fighting - a "terrible battle", the Colonel later called it - in which the Commandos held firm despite considerable losses, the Germans eventually withdrawing. A military history later stated:

Through the village of Dragonea and across the surrounding slopes, the din of battle could be heard. Charging with grenades and bayonets, the triumphant panzers of Major Fitz's battalion drove back the elite Commandos with reckless courage. Spent cartridges, rifle clips, ammunition boxes were strewn around the smoke-filled slopes. In the village a battered armoured vehicle blocked a narrow lane, a half-demolished house was in flames. Commandos and Panzers fought with ferocity on the hillsides and in the alleyways beneath a plaque commemorating Dragonea's dead in World War One. (Hickey & Smith, *Operation Avalanche*)

A description by 2 Commando's Harry Blissett, who directed the battle from the H.Q. on the hill, was similarly graphic:

Their columns came on, shouting their heads off, in single file-tommy gunner ahead and grenade men throwing grenades as a sower sows wheat. It was a grim struggle. Attack after attack was put in under a murderous mortar barrage and casualties streaming back to H.Q. told their own tale. H.Q. had its protective screen out and twice the enemy passed by on the right, but they never managed to consolidate ground gained. As fast as they came, they were pushed back. (*Salerno Diary*, 1944)

The focus of Jos' own account is more on the friends and comrades he lost: his bren-gunners, two young lance-corporals, Don Fermoy and Tony Shemmonds; Sergeant Hill (to whom he'd lent the watch which he never saw again); Arthur Brunswick, so quietly effective in charge of the mortars; and the Colonel's second-in-command, Tom Lawrie:

I was called back by a shout from Major Tom Lawrie. '4 Troop report there's a tank over the other side in Cava firing at them.' He'd brought a wireless set with him from Headquarters and was going to get the mortars onto it. Together we moved under a cluster of small saplings. 'Don't bunch!', shouted Frank Mason from the cover of the shack. But it was too late. Two whip-cracks reverberated in sharp succession. Both went over where Tom Lawrie and I were sitting. But the next one didn't. Like a thunderclap it exploded in the leaves above us. I shook myself. I was all right. But Sergeant Hill wasn't . . . And then I glanced at Tom Lawrie. He had fallen back and was gurgling. I lifted him up to find a gaping wound in his throat. I frantically got out a First Field Dressing but even as I did I realised it would be little use as the blood was spurting out and I couldn't tie it anywhere near tight enough.

Jos had just given him a dose of morphine, when Lawrie died in his arms. Jos looked around. The scene of the shell blast seemed suddenly deserted. He tried the wireless, but it was useless, so he crawled over to the shack which Frank Mason was using as a temporary 6 Troop headquarters:

There was a figure slumped over the Troop wireless set. It was Frank. He had been killed as he sat on the top step. Beside him was the incomparable Smith.

It was the same incomparable Smith who had once called the odds for Frank Mason on Derby Day at Gibraltar.

Jos now had to take over what remained of 6 Troop. He had three bren gun teams left, one sergeant (out of 6) and an RSM. He sent a runner to H.Q. and the Colonel himself soon appeared. "Situation is tricky," 'Mad Jack' conceded, "but Morny's coming up." Morny would be taking over from Lawrie, he said, and bringing with him mortars and some of 1-3 Troops. Somehow, the mere mention of the impending arrival of Morny sounded immensely reassuring. Perhaps because of his association with the Iron Duke the quiet and shy Morny exuded an air of invulnerability. But it was probably the wireless messages sent by Frank Mason, rather than the Commandos' regrouping, which really turned the battle. For a storm of explosives, fired by an Allied Field Regiment, was soon striking the German lines, eliciting from Major Fitz a brave but useless retaliation:

Indifferent to the fire, the black-uniformed commander led his men forward, shouting *Sturm, sturm!* Then, stumbling, he fell as a red hot fragment ripped his thigh into a mess of bloodied flesh . . . Now the Germans faced the relentless counter-attack of the Commandos who fought their way over the hill and into the village. Unable to withstand their fire, the Panzers' resistance began to crack. They pulled back to secondary positions, leaving behind in the streets and on the slopes their dead and wounded . . . (Hickey & Smith, *Operation Avalanche*)

But their secondary positions were to be of little use. A "fearsome" barrage from Allied cruisers of pinpoint accuracy from a distance of eight miles pounded a position only 200 yards in front of Jos and the other commandos. He wrote of it:

Human beings simply couldn't live in that maelstrom of high explosive. There were no dugouts or concrete emplacements, no shelter of any kind. Realising the impossibility of their position, the Germans put up a Verey light, their gunners put down smoke, and they retired. Carefully we moved forward again. The ground was pockmarked with shell holes; the trees and bushes were charred, all the vines flattened. Eventually, as darkness returned, we were relieved.

In just one morning, a quarter of 2 Commando had perished. 6 Troop, which had started out at Gibraltar with over 50 men, was now down to a mere 15. Unsurprisingly, 13 September 1943 went down in commando history as 'Black Monday'.

The horror of that day would always be very real for the survivors. Yet so, too, its revelation of the generosity of the human spirit. Jos later heard, for example, of one small group of 2 Commando, who when walking in the main street of Dragonea during the battle came across two German paratroopers, their weapons slung across their backs, helping a badly wounded comrade. For a split second the two groups stared at each other. The commandos' fingers were already on the triggers when their N.C.O. called out, "No firing, lads", motioning to the Germans to keep going. One of the paratroopers gratefully raised his arm in acknowledgement as they vanished around a corner.

Jos and 6 Troop had been in the field for four continuous days since landing, without a proper night's sleep or any washing facilities. Despite the huge physical exertion they had received little food. ("It is a good plan," wrote Captain Harry Blissett in his Salerno summary, "to practise living with only one meal a day. At Salerno the troops were very hungry.") It was a great relief for them when fresh infantry took over their hard-won positions, safeguarding the Molina Pass, and they were able to make the short journey by lorry to the centre of Salerno, badly damaged but now more or less in the Allies' control, where there was hope of cleaning themselves up and getting some rest. It was an uncomfortable place to be, as Blissett's comments suggest:

During this day all the Commandos rested and washed their clothes. We wore every variety of civilian clothing, whilst our own were drying . . . There was intermittent shell fire on the town throughout the day, and endless reports came in from friendly Italians of German positions in the rear of the town . . . Orders had now come through, however, that many Italians were really German agents.

For Jos and the other 14 men of 6 Troop, the washing of clothes was not a possibility. The empty villa where they were to spend two nights had completely lost its water supply. Nor did it have any cooking facilities. Not that this worried them. They were too tired to eat. Instead, they gratefully slept and rested on the stone floor through much of this fifth day in Italy. Most nights, however, German hit squads infiltrated the town, so Jos, as Troop Leader, finding sleep impossible, lay awake, his pistol beside him, ready to give support to whomever he'd posted on guard. It was an opportunity, too, to thank God for his safety, and to pray for all those who had been less fortunate. If the commandos in training at Achnacarry had been sceptical about their young officer being a 'Bible Basher', the survivors of 6 Troop, anxiously at rest in their forlorn Salerno villa, were very much less so, taking reassurance and strength from his quiet lead.

# 17
## JOS AT SALERNO (II)

Jos spent much of the rest day in conferences with Jack Churchill, Morny, Harry Blissett and the other Troop commanders. He learned that though Salerno itself had been captured, Operation Avalanche was still in a critical situation. The Germans had merely been driven back to the foothills of the surrounding mountains, from where they still threatened the whole beachhead. And so, on the late morning of 15 September, while General Alexander was assuring Winston Churchill that "everything possible is being done to make Avalanche a success" and that "its fate will be decided in a few days", 2 Commando started out on a new mission, leaving Salerno in army trucks amid heavy German mortars. ("Each time the three-tonners changed gear, a fresh batch of bombs came down on us."). They were taken to Mercatello, a village two and a half miles east of the town, on the coast road, and from there they marched into the hills, where, at an extremely decrepit old farmhouse, Jack Churchill met them for a briefing.

The night before, he explained, the Germans had launched so successful a counter-attack on the Battalion holding the head of the valley that they had seized three prominent positions overlooking Allied defences ('41 Commando Hill', 'The Pimple' and 'White Cross Hill') and were now in a position to cut off the entire beachhead in Salerno. Somewhere up in the valley was a Company of the Oxfordshire and Buckinghamshire Light Infantry, "holding on by their eyebrows". 41 Royal Marine Commando would attack the hill called after them, a great crag three miles inland, overlooking the village of Piegolelle from the east. 2 Commando would secure Piegolelle itself plus the two other hills which overlooked it, The Pimple on the north-east and White Cross Hill to the south-west. Meanwhile, as they swept across country towards these important objectives, they would eliminate any enemy infiltrating the area.

Daylight began to fade as Morny led 1-3 Troops up the valley on the left and Jack Churchill 4-6 Troops on the right. They enjoyed some spectacular early successes, 4 Troop's Gordon Hemming almost single-handedly capturing 40 Germans, and 'Mad Jack', with his trusty Beretta in hand, even more. When they reached the main scene of operations, Jos and 6 Troop were given the job of re-occupying Piegolelle and preparing positions against possible counter-attack, while the other Troops headed for Pimple and White Cross Hills. Jos' job proved unexpectedly easy. The Germans had left, or so it seemed. In the course of forming a defensive perimeter around the village, however, Jos was surprised to hear what sounded like snoring coming from a farm shed. "Pigs or I-ties," whispered one of his men, but Jos's farmyard search revealed neither. Instead, he unearthed some very sleepy Germans:

Although it was now between 2.00 and 3.00 in the morning we got to work in earnest. Out of nooks and crannies the wretched Germans tumbled. The numbers mounted. Eventually the village disgorged 136 prisoners, without a shot being fired . . .

136 Germans captured by 15 commandos! Piegolelle also furnished 6 Troop with four German mortars and twenty machine-guns.

There was an altogether more serious German defence of The Pimple and White Cross Hill, and 2 Commando, having made little impression, returned back to the village. Panzer reinforcements were being sent into the area, and that dawn a German assault began on 2 Commando, dug in at Piegolelle. Allied reinforcements were scheduled to come up in due course, within 24 hours, but for the moment the Commandos were virtually all there was to prevent a German push down the valley to the Salerno beachhead. It was a hard, bitter rearguard action:

We noted the German machine-gun sites on the slopes of The Pimple from the muzzle flashes on range cards. As each one was pinpointed, the mortars were given the range and the direction. When the mortars opened fire, every bren and captured weapon would hurl abuse at the position. With the liberal supply we now had, the boys could afford to be generous. If the responsive mortar fire became awkward, we could move our machine-guns at will, for the original German slit trenches and our alternatives offered plenty of scope.

There was grim satisfaction for the weary commandos in winning this firefight. Later on, however, things went less well in the area of the two hills, as Harry Blissett was to chronicle:

Morning came with both sides sitting either side of the valley. Our Commando held Piegolelle village and the high ground to the east [41 Commando Hill] but were being very hard pressed by the enemy who were well dug in on the slopes of the opposite Pimple Hill. Prisoners told us that their orders were to fight to the last round and last man. Throughout the day the Commandos remained in action with their losses steadily mounting. It was during the attempt by 2 Troop to recapture a part of the Pimple that Captain the Duke of Wellington was killed leading a gallant attack on some well dug-in positions. Weapons found in the vicinity of the area showed that they had reached the trenches and I saw many dead when I visited the area later.

For a second consecutive evening 2 Commando were forced to withdraw to Piegolelle. There, before dawn, anti-tank mines were laid in the roadway and defensive positions dug. The loss of Morny weighed heavily with everyone. That night, as if in some sad gesture of salute to his old friend, 'Mad Jack' Churchill produced his bagpipes and played some familiar tunes into the still night.

The hills were pounded with Allied artillery fire the next day, and it was 41 Commando's turn to attempt to take the hills. The attacks ended in defeat and severe losses. Both commando units regrouped that night in and around Piegolelle. Even greater efforts were renewed the next day, their ninth in Salerno, as the capture of these hills was now imperative for the safe passage of the Allied army advancing from the south-east. All day the commandos harassed the Germans, with almost constant fire, and by the late afternoon, as two infantry companies arrived to relieve them, there was minimal fire coming back from the Germans. The battle was as good as won.

That night, their last in Piegolelle, was memorable for 'Mad Jack' and his inspirational music. Jos recalled:

I remember him that night craning over a map and a report by the light of a miserable candle, guttering into the blanket-covered table. Then, long after midnight, when he could stand things no longer, he reached into the corner for his bagpipes and marched up and down the main street of Piegolelle, playing them, absolutely enthralled. If martial music could ever stir the hearts of tired men, those melodies did.

The next day, Allied artillery efforts were redoubled and the hills finally fell. But 2 Commando by this time had returned to reserve positions at Mercatello. Operation Avalanche was at last turning in the Allies' favour, as reinforcements were being poured in to support the invasion. The commandos' job was done, and Jos and his fellow survivors, camping in a field at Mercatello, were visited by General Richard McCreery, Commander of 10 Corps, the British part of the whole Anglo-American assault, to be congratulated for all they had achieved. They had saved a critical situation at Piegolelle, his official report later stated, and helped to turn that situation to the advantage of the landing forces. But it had cost 2 Commando another 48 lives, with nearly 150 seriously wounded.

On Sunday 19 September, Jos was able to write a few lines home, the first time he had been able to manage anything since leaving Sicily. His message was very simple:

Your prayers are answered. I'm fit and well and in the best of health. So sorry I haven't been able to write for a fortnight . . . The Lord has indeed been good and provided me with answers to prayer. We had a pretty busy time, but all the while I had an amazing feeling of peace in the midst of war. What a glorious Saviour.

Shortly afterwards he was able to offer his thanks at an extempore Church parade held in an orchard just south of Salerno, as shells echoed from the hills behind the town, German eighty-eight guns pounded the main road about a mile away, and the odd aeroplane roared overhead.

2 Commando were a spent force, in need of rest and new recruits. On 23 September 1943, just as the Commander of the British 8th Army,

General Montgomery, arrived at Salerno, Jos and his comrades embarked on a tank-landing-craft for an uncomfortable journey back to Sicily. They hardly noticed the discomfort. The heavy loss of dear friends was on all minds. For Jos, the death of Morny was particularly bitter.

When 2 Troop painted the words 'The Dook's Boys' over the door of their billet in Gibraltar, it showed something of the affection in which he was held. The decadence of an outmoded Dukedom and the vindication of the hereditary system were not for him. Not living on the memories of the past or living into an age which he could not understand because it had outgrown him, Morny left behind an untarnishable memory. He died at the very summit of his powers. The epitaph on his simple tombstone, set unobtrusively in the midst of hundreds of others in the plain but orderly cemetery at Pontecagnano, summed him up: 'To Morny, the Happy Warrior.'

The mood, then, was sombre, on the journey back to Sicily. The sheer futility of war seemed overpowering. As they passed the volcanic island of Stromboli, Jos felt it strangely symbolic: "Nothing exists on the island, nothing at all. It is simply full of sound and fury, signifying nothing."

They landed at Milazzo, on Sicily's north coast. Nobody seemed to be expecting them, so they slept on the pebbled shore, a blanket apiece. They were picked up by American trucks the next day and taken across the island to billets in Catania, former Italian barracks, where the Special Services Brigade was slowly reformed. Jos found a big post awaiting him, including a parcel whose contents he could guess before opening: precious socks, newly-knitted by his grandmother. Among the 40 letters was one from home with the sad news that they would probably soon have to move out of Ades, the country house the Nicholls had been renting and which they all so much loved, as it had just been put up for sale. Jos responded:

I was distressed to hear the sudden developments re Ades and the fact that September 29th will be past by the time this reaches you. But, and it's a glorious 'but', we KNOW that ALL THINGS work together for (the eventual) good to them that love God. And for those remaining 5 days I know I will be joining you all in committing the whole question into His keeping. I can take no physical action about it out here, so I know that my personal opinion was not meant to have been a share in this crisis - but I know that even if a move is inevitable God will have provided some better thing (however it may seem at the moment) for us all.

He allowed himself just one comment about Salerno:

Perhaps you will have seen from the papers that Morny is missing, believed killed. He led a bayonet charge and has not been seen since. He was an amazingly quiet laddie as a rule, and except for his moustache the very last person you would expect as a soldier. But in battle he really was the goods.

Soon afterwards Jack Churchill briefly returned to Salerno on a very private mission. With soldiers from the Body Recovery Unit he drove up to The Pimple and began the gruesome search of mounds of earth, looking for Morny's body, anxious to give it proper burial. It would in all probability have been unidentifiable, but he had jotted down, as he always did, items by which recognition might be possible. In Morny's case these included a plaited belt with a metal clip, metal stars on his shoulder, an upper dental plate and the pipe and plain tobacco tin he always carried.

And by such identification they finally found him. On the very hilltop, under six inches of earth, close to the body of a German officer who had confronted him. It seemed to Churchill as if both had pulled the triggers of their pistols at the same moment. They found, too, by the size of his boots, the Sergeant-Major who had gallantly accompanied Morny on this last sortie, and saw to it that both bodies were taken to Salerno to be buried, temporarily, in a grass square near the town.

For Jos, resting in Catania, the days at Salerno seemed strangely "far away and hard to realize except as a bad dream". A letter from John Jeffreys' mother told of a memorial service at the Chapel of the Royal Hospital, Chelsea. But deep grief remained. "John's going," she commented, "is to us as though the sun had set." Jos was in touch, too, with Frank Mason's widow, Dorothy. "At present," she told him, "I'm working awfully hard just to try and stop myself going crazy." Jos had written to Stowe's headmaster, J. F. Roxburgh, about Morny. "He was, as you say, a person of outstanding kindness and gentleness," replied Roxburgh, "but the ancestral fire burned within him all the same." While at Catania, Jos learnt that a close school friend, an exact contemporary of his in Humphrey Playford's House, had recently been buried in the nearby cemetery, having been killed during the battle for the island.

Jos revisiting Salerno after the war

Amid all this post-battle trauma, Jos was particularly grateful for the regular relief of the official church parades, which took place in a whole series of unusual places - a hall in an Italian barracks, a local cinema, an Italian courtroom, a Fascist meeting room (with VIVA IL DUCE still painted on the walls), even a Fish Factory. His own efforts to gather together a small Bible fellowship had met with little success:

Sgt Douglas is still 'fervent in spirit serving the Lord' but the others have drifted off. We both pray earnestly, and we know you will join us, that they may return to the fold and find a new and lasting wonder in the glory of the Cross so that the 'things of earth grow strangely dim in the light of His Glory and Grace'.

There was encouragement, however, in late October, with news of a Lieutenant (Rex Beatty MC) who was running a daily Bible Study at an army base only a mile away. There Jos met three or four other Christian officers, and the clouds of discouragement lifted. "We all had a grand time," he told his parents, "and they've invited me to go on any evening."

# 18

# DAVID: CARRIER TRIALS

David was soon relishing his new post with the Service Trials Unit, alternating land-based work at the Fleet Air Arm station at Crail, on the Scottish east coast, with trials at sea on the carrier *Pretoria Castle*, based in the Clyde Estuary. As usual, he was reassuring in his letters to his parents, making light of the risks inherent in the job:

I really think I am the most lucky ever. (Of course, luck isn't the word.) The job is even more pleasing than I expected and should be extremely interesting. I am afraid they took me a bit too literally when I told them at the Admiralty how good I was . . . ! I meant to tell you in my last letter that this job is almost totally non–belligerent. It's interesting, but not at all of a dangerous nature . . .

David photographed on board *Pretoria Castle*.

At the start of this new posting David had made 50 deck landings and flown a total of 600 hours. By the time it was to end, two years hence, he had doubled his flying hours and made 500 day and night deck landings, many of them under deliberately difficult conditions. Not only were new inventions and ideas given practical tests, but take-offs and landings were made with simulated technical problems. The margins for error were always very slim, and its consequences most serious, a crash-landing of a propellor-driven plane often rupturing a fuel pipe and causing a fire. Some of the aircraft types David worked upon, moreover, were notoriously unsatisfactory. Much of his earliest work, for example, involved the fast but unforgiving Fairey Barracuda, designed to replace the Fleet Air Arm's Swordfish and Fulmar biplanes. The Barracuda had just become operational - it featured in the Salerno landings - but was suffering from a whole series of major problems. There were several unexplained crashes, killing experienced pilots. Heavy use of the rudder could precipitate a dangerous spin. There were leaks in the hydraulic system which for long defied a cure. And the plane's basic instability was eventually only cured by a complete tail-wing re-design.

It was not long before David had his first serious mishap on *Pretoria Castle*. He wrote carefully to his parents:

I suppose I am a little more skilful than I used to be, but that isn't saying much. I'm sorry to say that I'm also more apprehensive than I was, and that's saying rather a lot. I am reminded how two years ago I altered Psalm 121 v.8 for my particular needs: "The Lord shall preserve thy taking-off and thy landing-on from this time forth."

On this occasion, despite all the care, he had broken the tail wheel on landing, missed the arrestor wire, and ended up badly damaging his aircraft against the crash barrier:

No-one tried to blame me, but, strictly speaking, it was an error of judgement. It's a fairly frequent type of prang but it's annoying all the same.

When working at sea on the Pretoria Castle, David was in charge of 60 men. Apart from the pilots and aircrew, they were an inexperienced group, with an average age of only 20. They had mostly volunteered for service in the carrier after working with David at Crail: "One rather embarrassing but cheering aspect has been the large number of men from the squadron who have applied to come with me." There was clearly a happy atmosphere within the team, reflecting the overall care he took in maintaining good morale. On the Pretoria Castle he was for ever participating in games of deck hockey, for example, and back at Crail he generously offered coaching in basic subjects like Maths and English to help those who had struggled at school to make more of themselves in later life.

*Pretoria Castle*

The drama and excitements of flying off a carrier were balanced by more mundane duties in the necessarily highly-organised life-style involving the *Pretoria Castle's* full complement of over 400 people and 20 aircraft. One such account, written in October 1943, while Jos's commando unit continued to regroup in far-away Sicily, gives a good picture of the hum-drum, day-to-day side of naval life and David's splendidly detached attitude towards it:

A Firefly catching a wire as it lands on the *Pretoria Castle*

We've had quite a busy week, but now we're at anchor and I'm Officer of the Day. It's about 10.00 o'clock in the evening, and I'm sitting in the Wardroom Anteroom, writing on my knee. I have to be here, as every now and then a messenger comes in and hands me a message or a signal. I look at these thoroughly and say, 'Ah yes, thank you.' Of only 50% of these have I the faintest clue as to what they are about. However, experience has shown that this technique is infallible, and the only serious mistake one can make is to get worried about anything . . .

It's been a busy day. I emerged on deck to find everything going splendidly. Neither the Met Officer nor the Engineer Commander nor his hose were anywhere to be seen, and the motor cutter was riding happily from the port boom. I then went to the office where I wrote a letter to the Captain about the loss of my raincoat yesterday. My Observer had opened the aircraft window and let it fly out. While I was writing this plaintive appeal for a refund, in comes the gangway messenger. 'Excuse me, sir, the Quartermaster says the Medical Officer will not be requiring the boat after all.' 'Medical Officer? Are you sure you don't mean the Meteorological Officer?' 'Yes, sir. That's right.' 'Well, which do you mean?' 'The Met-what-you-said, sir.'

Then I cleared the In-tray. Demand forms for stores, requests for leave . . . The rest of the day was occupied with the usual things: lighters rudely honking for attention alongside; a waterboat and a burst pipe; libertymen; defaulters et cetera. Oh yes, the Captain did rounds during the morning. The hangar and the mess decks were a joy to look on. So, of course, he never came near them and inspected the storeroom and offices . . .

Rows of arrestor wires stretch across *Pretoria Castle*'s deck

David surrounded by his squadron's football team

David was equally at ease at Crail, where he had his own small cabin on the aerodrome and, for transport, a bicycle and motor-bike. The development work also involved him in a certain amount of interesting travel. On one particularly busy day he took off mid-morning from Crail in a Fairey Firefly (a 2-seater fighter just being introduced); stopped for lunch at Newcastle; did business in Liverpool; had supper at Northampton; changed planes at a tiny aerodrome called Heathrow; and flew back late at night to Scotland. ("The trip was absolutely glorious. What a funny little island we do live in!") There were less good days, when traces of the fever he had picked up in Africa returned and he found himself easily tired.

The hours were long, too, and the work inherently stressful. On one occasion, when he was Aerodrome Control Officer at Crail, a young pilot disappeared on a routine night-time training flight. When the rest of the aircraft landed at around 2.00 a.m. and he heard the bad news, David duly informed coastal command and the coastguard and then waited and waited by the telephone. As dawn began to break, he looked out across the concrete runway and noticed a Fulmar of his own squadron. Searches for missing aircraft were governed by various rules and much red tape relating to petrol restrictions. Planes in the sea tended, anyway, to be like proverbial needles in haystacks. The Fulmar, however, was half-full of petrol and on the spur of the moment, his tiredness completely forgotten, David took it off on a search. The sea was utterly calm, without a ripple. He flew at just 200 feet, observing careful patterns over the area where, he estimated from the reports, the plane might have crashed. But the longer he searched, the more pointless it seemed. He was just about to return to Crail, when he spotted something different. He flew lower and lower, and, for a split second, there indeed was something white and yellow on a dark background. Noting its position, he sped back to the airfield and alerted Coastal Command's Anson patrol. The Anson, following David's instructions, discovered that "the white and yellow blur" was, in fact, a young pilot, lying on the detached, floating wheel of his lost aircraft. He had been in the sea several hours and was semi-conscious when found. But then disaster! The glassiness of the early morning sea deceived the Coastal Command's pilot, and he too crashed. Miraculously, however, a small fishing boat came to the Anson crew's rescue and both they and the semi-conscious pilot were brought safely to the shore.

There was a remarkable sequel. Visiting the pilot in hospital, David discovered that he too was a member of the Officers' Christian Union (now the Armed Forces' Christian Union), had known that David was also a member, but had been too shy to introduce himself.

This revelation was a reminder of what a struggle Christian witness at Crail had been proving. For some time David had been feeling very bewildered about it. The Sunday services at the station, in particular, were very poorly attended. "I'm ashamed to say," he confessed to his parents, "that I've done nothing about Christian work here", adding enigmatically, "It would, I think, be considerably easier if there were no chaplain …"

Soon after the Firefly rescue mission, however, an opportunity for action arose with the establishment of Air Training Corps camps at Crail. In addition to giving students rides in an old Swordfish, David also played a leading part in the organisation of their services and sometimes spoke to them of his own faith. In one of these A.T.C. talks, he attributed "every single thing" in his life which had been "worth anything" to Jesus, assuring his listeners "how completely adequate my Saviour has been in meeting my needs". After giving some examples of this, he concluded powerfully:

What but the gospel of Jesus can meet such needs? Lovingly, but urgently, I commend my Saviour to you. Everything I've seen in the war has convinced me afresh that His claim to be 'the way, the truth and the life' is absolutely true. The world is rushing on, our lives are rushing by, 'the day is far spent'. Not one of us here can afford to reject His claim on our lives.

This work with the A.T.C. camps at Crail was the start of a lifelong involvement of sharing his faith with young people. Another such surviving talk, given after the war was well over, specifically referred back to his time with the Service Trials Unit:

One of my jobs was helping in the selection of suitable pilots for carrying out certain flying trials. What were the qualities one hoped to see in these trials pilots?

First, the ability to get on with others: *love*. Then cheerfulness, the good-humoured sort which spreads to others: *joy*. Coolness, the ability to consider problems, difficulties and dangers quietly and accurately: *peace*. Patience, good temper when things go wrong, when other people are irritated or anxious: *long-suffering*. Soft speaking, not loud-mouthed or line-shooting, but tactful and considerate: *gentleness*. Then honesty, truthfulness in making reports, a real keenness to do the job well: *goodness*. Loyalty, both to superiors in rank and to principles - to safety precautions, to high standards of care; confidence in people and things: *faith*. Humility - not doing anything to bring credit on oneself: *meekness*. And finally reasonableness and lack of excess in all things: *temperance*.

There's a list of these qualities in slightly different words in Galatians 5, verses 22-23: "But the fruit of the Spirit is love, joy, peace, long-suffering, gentleness, goodness, faith, meekness, temperance; against such there is no law." Note, they are the fruits (or results) of the Spirit, the Holy Spirit, which Jesus Christ has promised will come to those who trust themselves entirely to Him. I wouldn't think of suggesting these fine qualities to you, if I didn't know one sure way in which you can learn them. Through Jesus Christ ...

The taking of air cadets on joyrides in a Swordfish and the organizing of services for them were pleasant, occasional diversions from the remorseless, day-to-day efforts of aeronautical development and testing. For his first seven months in the job, from April to November 1943, David worked without leave, steadily building up 'B Flight' and its reputation. It was both rewarding and exhausting. Apologising to his parents for lack of letters, he explained: "I have had little energy for anything but the job, which is never finished. It has gone really wonderfully well and I have absolutely everything to be thankful for."

In the war, good news was at last beginning to mix with the bad. "This bombing is an awful and solemn thing," he wrote of the massed air raids now taking place on German industrial sites and cities. "It is almost more saddening than when we were suffering it ourselves." He greeted the fall of Sicily with delight, and the news that at long last the Allies, through the landings at Salerno, were pushing forwards towards Naples and Rome. "We have so much to thank God for. It's hard to know how to take such good news after so long ..."

In November 1943, a visit to London for discussions at the Admiralty allowed David a short leave, part of which he spent at Ades with the Nicholls (who had managed to solve the crisis over the sudden sale of the house by buying it themselves). Joanna was now a student nurse at Mount Vernon Hospital, Hayward's Heath. While David was staying at Ades, as luck would have it - or so he was led to believe - one of the Nicholls' two Vauxhalls needed servicing in Hayward's Heath, so David volunteered to take it there, and he and Joanna were able to meet up again. They spent the best part of the day together, first at the local zoo and later at that most popular entertainment of the period, a newsreel cinema. Some of the war footage moved David to tears, but, as he reported afterwards, "I don't think that Joanna saw, so it was all right."

Inevitably their conversations were dominated by the latest family news. Joanna had recently received a letter from Jos. He was "safe and well" in Sicily, apparently, after "a busy time". He was likely, she said, to be in southern Italy that Christmas. After which, he could go simply anywhere . . .

# 19
## JOS IN YUGOSLAVIA

Jos and 2 Commando remained in Sicily long enough for 'Mad Jack' to be able to organise a training assault on the rim of Mount Etna's smoking volcano, and then, on 6 November 1943, transferred from Catania to Molfetta, a coastal town in southern Italy, just north of Bari, the journey (with Jos as Baggage Officer) proving an agonisingly cold experience, a rain-swept voyage to Taranto followed by "an initiation into the miseries of the Italian State Railways".

Further torrential rain ("buckets and buckets of it") made the early days in south Italy a trial, but Molfetta, with its pink, flat-roofed houses, pretty harbour and ancient churches dedicated to obscure saints, was to prove an attractive temporary base for Christmas and the New Year as 2 Commando continued their recruitment and training programme. Rejoicing in their freedom from the Nazis, the locals were determined to turn every weekend into a new fiesta. "Today being Sunday," Jos reported, "the town is in a ferment over a fair." The main piazza was a-glitter with swings and merry-go-rounds. Wine flowed freely. It was all oddly unreal.

His first job was to train up a new Troop, named 'the Wellington' after Morny, and to give an 'Achnacarry briefing' to potential instructors of three further new Troops, 'the Broome', 'the Brunswick' and 'the Mason'. By January 1944 'the Wellington' was in good shape and Jos was cheerfully putting 'the Broome' through its paces with a heavy emphasis on speed marches.

One regular companion at Molfetta was Pat Henderson, who had won the MC at Salerno and been promoted to Acting Brigade Major:

Pat is great fun and keeps us in line with the latest dope. He told us yesterday that the Allied Military Government for Occupied Territories (or AMGOT), which we met rather too much of in Sicily, stood for Amateur Military Gentlemen on Tour! The award of the OBE was for Other Blighters' Efforts and the MBE for Much Base Experience . . .

Their sporting enthusiasm was another bond:

Yesterday I saw a rugger ball! A real live one. I whipped it up and rushed away with it. It's blown up and quite new-at least it was until Pat called me out after my run for a spot of kicking up and down the main road outside our mansion. We've been searching around for a field but there isn't a field with grass this side of the Alps as far as I can see!

Jos had again been made the unit's Sports Officer - hence the search for suitable pitches. Eventually they settled for an unpromising little clearing among the ubiquitous olives, and he was just supervising the making of goals and clearing of stones when an attack of mild jaundice forced him to spend three weeks in an Army hospital.

It proved a helpful period of reflection, an opportunity for taking stock of things, and while he was in the hospital, enjoying the luxury of linen sheets and real beds, he mused on what he might do if he survived the war.

I'm thinking seriously of being a parson - it is very hard to imagine. Wearing a perpetual dog collar etc.! But I think that it would wear off soon enough. And it would be rather fun to be a school chaplain - if one could get the job. Anyway, I get a lot of fun thinking about it.

He had currently been studying Nehemiah and finding the writings of King Artaxerxes' resourceful wine-taster remarkably relevant to his present situation:

In one chapter he gives the action of the Christian in attack and in defence. In defence: "We made our prayer unto our God and set a watch against them day and night." (4 v.9) And in attack: "Remember the Lord, which is great and terrible, and fight." (4 v.14) Nehemiah was a great tactician with a very cute eye for strategy as well . . .

At 23, Jos was extremely volatile, and quite different from the avuncular figure of his later years. "Would God the typical Commando was more Christ-like," he wrote at this period, "and the typical Christian more commando-like!" The viewpoint made him quite critical of other approaches to faith, particularly high church. Attending a Presbyterian Service near Molfetta, he criticised a Welsh Padre for being "rather too intellectual". And he was horrified to hear that his old housemaster, the Revd Humphrey Playford, had just "had the effrontery" to put a cross and candles on the altar in the Stowe School chapel, "where simplicity was the very essence of its beauty and its fascination for me". He was becoming similarly critical of the Army's compulsory Sunday services with their lack of hard-hitting sermons and emphasis on Army ritual :

How I've got to loathe Church Parades - I used to wonder whether they didn't do some good, but now I very much doubt it. There is too much Drill Square and Polishing Up for it . . . They've abolished Sick Parades and I think they should set about 'de-regimentalising' Church Parades.

Yet he still nursed some sympathy for church ceremony. When his young sister Charitie wrote from home that she preferred the sermons at the local Mission Hall to those in Chailey Church, he totally agreed. "Would that we could combine the two to the extent of bringing the Sanctity of worship into contact with the Saving power of the Word."

Just as he had criticised in Sicily the sermons of the Padre (a future Canon and headmaster of some distinction) for being "lacking in power" and failing to make their points with clarity ("like so many schoolmasters"), so too Jos was less than impressed by their new Padre in Molfetta, a 30-year-old Cambridge graduate, Gareth Banting, the son of a vicar of a gentle country parish outside Nottingham. Banting was a shy young man, with pronounced high church leanings:

Our padre has arrived with us. I was able to borrow a book or two from him - including Plato's *Republic*. He showed me some very wishy-washy pamphlets so I produced *Practical Christianity* for him! He seemed quite interested, so I told him about the O.C.U. (He asked quite politely if it was anything to do with the Oxford Group!) I do hope it may be possible to follow this up when I get back. It is so very hard to work solely through the troops - and there's nothing like being able to work through the Padre . . .

His disappointment in Banting did not lessen in the coming months:

—I'm afraid our St George's Day service - a week late - wasn't as good as yours. The Padre spoke for 15 minutes on St George being a good legendary figure and ourselves also being good and fighting dragons. But there was never the slightest thought of SIN. As you suggest, mother dear, Monty's opinion of the Padres' possibilities and their worth is very high, but I'm afraid very few live up to it . . .

—Since Gib I have met nobody (except Rex Beatty) and no organisation with any Good News to proclaim. In fact, for 6 months I have been unable to unburden myself to anyone - and that is something I find very hard. There are 2 lads in another Troop of the Commando who are searching, but they have to do it all through the Padre - and he is about as keen as a rusty pen-knife. He has been persuaded to start a small Bible Study class but he has let it fall through and doesn't want me there.

The Padre, clearly, struggled to relate to Jos's volatility, and the sad gap between them meant that Jos went his own way, and the hopes he nursed at Molfetta for developing a Christian fellowship were dashed when the commando who had once stood up for the Bible in the Sergeants' Mess was invalided home.

As more recruits arrived for Jos to train up, familiar faces continued to recede, Harold Blissett being another loss to 2 Commando as he returned to England to take up a staff college position. Pat Henderson, too, had departed, seconded back to the Royal Engineers, as part of the British 8th Army which, with the US 5th Army, was about to mount a massive attack on heavily entrenched German positions north of Naples. Nonetheless Jos was in good heart as he spent Christmas in Molfetta:

Church Parade for all units in the town at 10.00 in the local cinema. Lesson reading from Luke and some grand old Christmas hymns. It sent me back to each of the last four Christmas Day services:

1939: that grand walk across the fields at Chailey to St Peter's. How I love the good old C. of E. service in a country church (I'll be a padre yet!) 1940: a Church Parade from the barracks to Shrivenham village with a full church and good singing. 1941: Tackly Church, near Oxford - a very small congregation but a typical Christmas with snow on the ground. Then an excellent dinner with the vicar! 1942: Service at Holy Trinity, Ayr. A full congregation but rather too theoretical a sermon - and a lovely carol service in the afternoon. And now 1943 in an Italian cinema, with the service taken by the C. of E. Padre and a very short sermon by the Royal Marine Padre.

Somehow a wonderful Christmas lunch was concocted for 2 Commando at which, by tradition, the officers served the men. That evening there was a Commando concert, 'Green Berets-Second Bunch', a follow-up to the one Frank Mason and John Jeffreys had concocted in Gibraltar, one of the highlights being 'Mad Jack' on his bagpipes.

Shortly afterwards their extrovert Colonel travelled 120 miles up the Adriatic to hold secret negotiations on the island of Vis, off the Dalmatian coast, with the supporters of the Yugoslavian freedom fighter, Josip Broz Tito. Vis might only be small - just 18 miles long and 8 miles wide - but, as the most outerly-lying of a series of small islands off the Dalmatian coast, just north of Dubrovnik, it was strategically very important. The Italian army had been occupying Dalmatia, and after Italy's withdrawal from the war the islands were not immediately re-taken by the Germans, so they had quickly become a rallying place and refuge for the Partisan cause. Tito's ad hoc army, made up largely of peasant farmers, had been causing the Nazis and Italians great irritation, but he was currently under considerable pressure, on the run in the Bosnian mountains. If, as the Allies now believed, Tito's Partisans were the country's best hope for Yugoslavia's post-war future, then it was important he be supported in every possible way.

Jack Churchill's quick visit to Vis helped seal an agreement that British and American Special Service troops, as many as a thousand, would be sent to help the partisans defend the Dalmatian islands from the likely threat of German invasion. But by the time the first four Troops of 2 Commando sailed north, in mid-January 1944, all the Dalmatian islands, excepting Vis, had been recaptured. Vis, therefore as the Allies' single foothold in the Balkans, became even more strategically important.

Jos was initially left behind, to his great disappointment ("Blinking Base Wallah, Admin. Archie, that's me . . .") to continue training up the last two

Troops. He accordingly missed the first of attempts of 'Mad Jack' to give the Germans something to think about - a series of hit-and-run raids on nearby islands.

The disappointment soon evaporated. Jos was a natural instructor:

I'm having a glorious time training the new intake. They are very keen and eager to learn. I'm only afraid that I shoot rather a big line. I found myself lecturing for an hour and five minutes on Commando history last night - laying it on with a trowel. And then after another full day's work spoke for 55 mins. tonight on Fieldcraft! Tomorrow it is on the Prismatic Compass! After an 8-mile march.

But there was news in mid-January which took away all the fun of training the recruits. Pat Henderson had just died in a Naples hospital of wounds suffered not far from Monte Cassino. The Hendersons' Sussex home was close to that of the Nicholls, and Pat's younger brother had been Jos's contemporary at Stowe. It was hard to believe that Pat Henderson's "quiet but forceful character, which made him extremely popular with everybody he met" would be enlivening no more lives.

The loss of one Stowe friend was followed by the arrival of another, a South African, Mike Webb, who had been with the 8th Army in Africa. Webb, who was a little older than Jos, had won the MC at El Alamein, where he had been wounded, and then served as A.D.C. to General Robertson, Montgomery's chief administrative officer. A non-stop talker, Webb proved immense fun, and Jos and Dickie Hooper were delighted to enrol him in their own Troop:

He likes to give you the impression, as most of these 8th Army blokes do, that there's no fighting like a desert tank battle! All very much in the fashion of a day out hunting! Tally ho! He always talks as though he were a Brigade Commander! So our whole conversation is now controlled from such a standpoint. (To collect rations from the NAAFI you send a Corps in with Div. Artillery support, plenty of fighter cover and a spot of 10 in. cruiser shelling!) Now that he's a subaltern in the Commando it is impossible to realise that Monty, Alexander, Tedder and all the other big noises knew him as 'Mike' . . .

After the training programme had reached an exhilarating conclusion with manoeuvres in the snowy Apennines, Jos and Mike Webb brought the new intake up the Adriatic to rejoin 2 Commando, a slow, uncomfortable journey from the southern Italian port of Manfredonia. It was the evening of 12 February 1944:

The ship was loaded with supplies of all sorts - food for the garrison, clothing and weapons for the Partisans. Partisans who had been wounded and were now returning to fight jostled with sinisterly bearded Liaison Officers in the saloon. There was a real cloak and dagger atmosphere.

Jos noted that among those returning to Vis was a young girl who, despite having lost an arm, was determined to continue the struggle against the Germans. It was after midnight when the *Lublijana* sailed round the island towards its north-eastern corner, where it entered the harbour of Vis, approached by a long lagoon and protected by clusters of mines. A shot was fired from the cliffs, the bullet whistling across the bows; a signal was hastily flashed from the ship's bridge to reassure the defenders; and the *Lublijana* steamed ponderously through to the small inner bay, rocky crags on either side. As soon as the heavily-laden ship put in, a searchlight was switched on and a horde of partisans rushed on board to start a rapid unloading.

There was a 3-ton truck waiting to take Jos and 5 Troop through the mountains on the island's only passable road, round many a hairpin bend, to where they were to be based - the island's second, and only other, harbour, Komiza, on the west coast, a little town nestling underneath the uncompromising mass of Mount Hum, rising sheer out of the sea to nearly 2,000 feet.

Their enthusiastic reception at Komiza belied the time - it was 2 o'clock in the morning - and Jos found himself ushered courteously into the local schoolroom, which was just being cleaned by "a whole army of women". His room boasted "a magnificent double bed and dainty lace curtains". Despite this unaccustomed luxury, a few hours later he woke up in alarm to the steady tramp of goose-stepping feet outside his window:

It could only be Germans! Surely nobody else marched quite like that. Suddenly, as they approached, they burst out into song. It was one of those haunting marching songs of the Dalmatian Brigade, which I came to know so well, *Domo Vina* ('My Fatherland').

Major-General Tom Churchill, 'Mad Jack''s elder brother, who was currently on Vis himself as the officer commanding the whole Commando Brigade of which 2 Commando was just a part, was later to write of the partisans:

Singing appeared to be one of the few pastimes they indulged in. Any meeting they attended, any luncheon held to celebrate anything, was always punctuated by the singing of these songs, nearly always unaccompanied. Any member present, man or woman, would start a song, and the rest would at once take it up and sing with the utmost gusto. Many of the songs were sung to Russian tunes - modern Red Army marching songs - with Yugoslav themes in the Yugoslav language. Several were mournful, and dealt with the hardships of their country and their folk ... (*Commando Crusade*)

1-3 Troops were stationed in Vis itself, while 4 and 5, along with 'Mad Jack', Commando H.Q. and Royal Navy liaison, were at Komiza. 2 Commando's Heavy Weapons Troop, specially brought for the defence of the island, was housed between the two sites, at a hamlet with an unpronounceable named, re-christened 'Duck Splash Farm'. It was uncompromising terrain. The island was nothing but bare rock, olive trees, clumps of pruned vines and hard evergreen shrub, but the locals everywhere were immensely welcoming. One of Jos' landladies gave him an insight as to why. Shortly before the Italians had surrendered, some Partisans from Komiza had surprised an Italian outpost, killing an Italian soldier. The local Italian commander had ordered, by way of reprisal, the first ten men found in Komiza to be rounded up and shot. Among them was the landlady's brother, the local priest.

But there was little time for talk. The German 118 Division was now concentrated on the nearest large island to them, Korkula. Another German Division was known to be in the Dubrovnic area with a spare regiment. An invasion of Vis was expected any moment, and for Jos's first week on the island, 2 Commando spent the nights in battle positions on the central plain with a motley group of Partisans, ready to counter-attack in the direction of any German thrust. Against impossibly uneven odds, their defence of the island was likely to end in bloody failure. Two days into their stay on Vis, Jos at last completed a letter home which he had started back in Molfetta. "So sorry for the delay," he commented calmly. "It has been rather hard to settle down to a letter just recently."

2 Commando's headquarters on the island of Vis

2 Commando were continuing to combine possible defence with very real offence - via further hit-and-run raids - partly to convince the Germans that the forces on Vis were much stronger than they were, and partly to divert German resources away from their continuing push on the mainland against Tito. The island of Solta was 'Mad Jack''s next objective, its position a particularly strategic one, protecting the entrance to the port of Split. His briefing made it sound simple: 4 troops of 2 Commando and 100 men of the U.S. Special Operations Group were to land in the middle of the night - in daytime there was too much danger from German planes - and surround the town of Grohote in the centre of Solta, closing to within 500 yards of the town. Then the Heavy Weapons Section would let fly with everything they had (mountain guns, mortars and heavy machine-guns), and 36 RAF Kittyhawk fighter-bombers

would suddenly materialise and bomb the German garrison, after which the commandos would rush in. Having caused 24 hours of maximum mayhem, they would rush out again and be picked up the next night by the same landing craft which had brought them in. Jos and 5 Troop were to take responsibility for the safety of the RAF's Ground Controller (whose understanding of what was going on in the island and contact, via radio, with the dive-bombers was absolutely crucial).

Three large landing craft duly reached Tatinja Cove on the southern coast of the small island around midnight:

Everything was so eerily quiet that the loudest sound was the echo of the boats' motors barely ticking over as they were carried forward under their own momentum. The entrance to the cove was very narrow and the beach inadequate to take the landing craft, which had to moor alongside an extremely precipitous and rocky slope. As the assaulting troops disappeared upwards into the darkness, they kicked tiny pieces of flint-like rock off the zig-zagging path. As these fell, they tinkled in a fascinating way, like cowbells in a distant Swiss pasture.

There was also, inevitably, a certain amount of noise from manhandling the big guns, in bits and pieces, up the cliffs, and then putting them together at the top.

Fortunately, the Germans were too far away to hear, and by dawn the commandos were in position, circling the town of Grohote in a 500-yard radius, having dealt with several enemy outposts. All went smoothly. Jos's Troop, safely escorting the key RAF personnel and Churchill's H.Q. team, only had one mischance:

The radio set had been put up, but it was altogether impossible to disguise the vast aerial that went with it. At 6.00 a.m. the heavy weapons opened up and so too did the loudspeaker of our propaganda unit . . . The effect of the latter was that a German mortar bomb landed just above it. Colonel Jack was speaking at the time . . .

Further mortar fire would probably have done for them, but just at that moment, right on cue, the 36 Kittyhawks arrived, each plane dropping its bombs with precision, though the commandos waiting to make the final attack, taking cover behind stone walls, trees and bushes, were sprayed with debris. So effective was the bombing that there were few Allied casualties in the subsequent attack, and over 100 survivors from the German garrison were rounded up. They and the raiding party were duly picked up by the Royal Navy that night and taken back to Vis.

The raid successfully bothered the Germans, who responded by tripling Solta's garrison and putting in concrete gun emplacements, mines and barbed wire. Air-raids followed on Vis, every house in Komiza being hit or damaged. A subsequent attack with incendiary bombs highlighted German displeasure. But they cautiously held back from a full-scale invasion.

2 Commando, as a matter of policy, made light of the Germans' control of the sky, so Jos was as busy as ever in the organisation of sporting relaxations, however primitive. Occasional games of rugger, for example, made do with soccer goalposts, and a mock gymkhana featured an officers' jeep race (in which 'Mad Jack' Churchill drove with particular gusto), a race on mules and a concluding song and dance routine from the locals. Sometimes, in leisure moments, they simply behaved as if on a peacetime holiday. One afternoon Jos, in the company of Mike Webb and three other officers, rowed out to "a cosy cove, beached the dinghy and then just sat on the rocks or dived into the water". Jos' matter-of-fact description - with the sea "anything but warm" and the sun "gloriously hot" - made it all sound rather like Clacton.

In addition to further raids on German-held islands, 2 Commando now began a new activity with the Partisans: night-time attacks on Axis' shipping. This was the idea of one of the most flamboyant of wartime heroes, a young Canadian, Captain Tom Fuller, whose legendary exploits in swift gunboats gave him the nickname 'The Pirate of the Adriatic', and who, in March 1944, first took up residence in Komiza harbour with his flotilla of six vessels. Fuller, who during the war survived the loss of no less than 13 gunboats he was commanding, had done a deal with the delighted 'Mad Jack' to attack and commandeer enemy vessels plying the Dalmatian coast at night, so that the Partisans themselves could add them to their fleet. The commandos would supply Fuller with the boarding parties.

It was not long before Jos and 5 Troop were answering this call, and Jos was later to write a vivid account of his first such expedition, in early

April. There were two gunboats on this occasion, the first led by Tom Fuller himself.

They were superb-looking little craft with glorious lines. They carried a small, quick-firing gun, twin Lewis guns on the bridge and depth charges. My party of 6 men were on board the second craft, following Tom Fuller's in line astern. As we shot out of Komiza harbour in the twilight, heading north, we put on speed. Hitting the swell further out, we rolled and bounced. I stuck it out on the bridge as long as I could ...

For a long time, off the coast of Dalmatia, they searched for prey in vain. They were just beginning to think that the coming daylight would force them home, as they made their final reconnaissance in enemy waters:

As we crept into the next bay, almost imperceptibly the tall masts of a ghostly-looking schooner came round the headland in front. The suspense was terrible. Moving desperately slowly, as though part of the backcloth itself, the whole bulk of the schooner became silhouetted against the rising moon. Still no-one stirred. The crew were waiting for Tom to give the word and he was motionless. Suddenly I saw why. Behind the schooner, and menacingly lethal, came a German E boat. It was perfectly outlined. Our two gunboats had come in line abreast. Without a tremor in his voice, Tom said, 'E boat ahead. All guns, fire!' They belched fire and flame. The tracer hit the water close astern of the E boat, and then smack into its hull. The concentrated fire of the two craft was enough. Before the E boat could even traverse her guns, the fire had started, spurts of flame and smoke prefacing an explosion. Still the gunboats fired. German sailors were jumping, falling or being flung overboard. Then the E boat seemed to buckle up, erupt in a cascade of water, and – each part of her fantastically scissored – she slipped beneath the now placid surface of the sea.

As the E boat sank, Tom Fuller yelled across the waters to Jos, "You deal with the schooner!" Down on deck, Jos readied his small band of boarders.

It was impossible to decide how tall the schooner was. Would we need to jump down or clamber up? Coming in on her port quarter (the ideal position), our gunboat grazed the schooner's side. "Boarders away!" On giving this time-honoured shout, I reached up for the schooner's gunwale and scrambled over the side.

The frightening appearance of Jos and his six men clambering over the gunwale was too much for the Germans manning the schooner's gun who had jumped overboard in panic. Racing into the deckhouse, Jos discovered two Yugoslavian seamen, only too ready to carry out his orders. Soon the schooner, which was transporting grain, was in tow, and with Jos standing guard over the seamen, it groaned under the strain of its engine on maximum power, the hold starting to ship water from the unaccustomed buffeting it was receiving. The gunboat eased its pace, the commandos took turns working the pumps, and somehow the unlikely journey back to Vis was successfully completed. As they entered the harbour they lowered the ship's Nazi flag and put up a tattered Red Ensign.

Despite the early hour, there was a big crowd on the quay as they put in. They had been lucky. Another gunboat, returning from a similar mission, had been attacked by two Messershmitts with the loss of six lives. The Partisans delightedly joined the Navy in unloading the schooner's stores, not just the useful grain, but the Germans' sauer-kraut and cigarettes also proving very popular. Jos, however, was very quick in one direction. "We have just managed to acquire some really superb Danish butter," he wrote joyfully home, "and have very nearly made ourselves sick on it. We've just got to eat it all up before it goes bad – and it is just like cream!"

The Partisans were delighted to be given the schooner and insisted on a handing-over ceremony, for which a visiting British naval V.I.P. was hastily produced. The Partisans' band, however, having given a nimble rendition of 'The Red Flag', found the melodic line of the National Anthem difficult to sustain, even at funereal pace. Meanwhile, all eyes were on the schooner's masthead, where the Red Ensign was being lowered and the Partisan flag raised. Jos was alarmed to see the two flags meeting and getting stuck together halfway up, the V.I.P.s still rigidly saluting and the National Anthem droning onwards:

In the nick of time a mere scrap of a boy took it into his head to dash forward, push aside the seaman, and shin up the mast like a monkey. Nothing could have been better timed or staged. As the flags were shaken free, the band, with a painful effort, reached the last bars and the situation, pregnant with international complications, was saved.

Such entertaining ceremonies were a much-needed diversion for the Partisans from their own terrible fighting. When they raided the island of Mljet, for example, they overran the whole German garrison. Over 300 Germans were killed and 800 taken prisoner, a particularly high number, as neither side usually offered the other the rules of the Geneva Convention. The killing of prisoners was common. Yugoslavia, moreover, was a country torn apart by bitter internal divisions which the Nazi occupation had exacerbated, leading to terrible mass genocide. (Out of the one and three-quarter million people who perished in the country in the course of the war, a million were Yugoslavs killed by fellow Yugoslavs.)

Jos's next Dalmatian challenge was to accompany a party of Partisans (30% of them women) on a raid of the nearby island of Korcula, Jos and seven of his men looking after a radio donated by the British. One afternoon in late April, therefore, Jos and his group were taken by lorry to Vis, where he met the Partisan leader, Tito's staunchest and most aggressive general, Colonel Zuljevic, whose heroism had already lost him the use of his left eye, right arm and left leg, but whom Jos found still bubbling with enthusiasm. The harbour was crammed with schooners of every shape and size. By nightfall a huge armada was ready to convey around 2,000 fighters, who set off to noisy acclaim from the quayside. To Jos, the uncontrolled exuberance was extremely alarming:

As one half of the armada split off, just outside the harbour, they fired their personal weapons. The noise of the firing added to the shouting and the singing, and the whole thing seemed ridiculous. With the German-held islands clearly visible to the north, there seemed to be no attempt to achieve surprise, and nobody tried to control the bedlam.

In the event, the two-pronged, three-day attack on the Germans garrisoned at Korcula proved remarkably successful, culminating in the largest German surrender the Partisans had yet experienced. For Jos, however, there was a shocking reminder of the atrocities which were being perpetrated in this campaign, notably by the Ustase, the pro-German Croatian fascists, whose concentration camps were filling with their racially-unacceptable fellow-countrymen. It occurred early on in the expedition, before they reached the chief city of Blato:

Yugoslavian partisans off the coast of Vis

The Partisans brought in a prisoner. He was searched in front of me and a couple of photographs were found. One of these showed a group of Germans and Ustase, standing in front of a pile of bodies. Some of the 15-20 bodies were mangled, most were of men, but some were women and youths. They had simply been piled up like animal carcases, ready to be thrown into a common grave. Looking again at the photo, I noticed that the shooting party were leaning on their rifles or shot guns, just as though they had come back from a grouse moor and some were grinning proudly.

The other photograph was even more repellent. Later the same evening, Jos asked where the prisoner was, to be told that he had met with an accident . . .

Subsequently, in Blato, on the third night of the operation, there was an incident involving a captured Ustase youth:

He was tied by the arms and legs by wire and had cuts on his face and neck from which blood was pouring. Three Partisan women, armed with rifles, thereupon clubbed him as he lay helpless.

Outraged, Jos made a bitter complaint to an interpreter, only to be told that the youth had been a criminal who had hung a Partisan from a tree on the green. Deeply upset, Jos persevered, eventually confronting General Zuljevic himself, who, as usual, was grinning happily.

I explained that if the British were to support the Partisans, we had to have an assurance that prisoners would be treated according to the Geneva Convention. "Yes, yes, of course," came back the answer from the interpreter. "The General agrees."

Later, Jos took the issue up at the highest level on the British side. There was little to be done, he was told, bar another stern, but probably useless, demand for proper treatment of prisoners.

The sudden possibility of the unit being parachuted into mainland Yugoslavia led to Jos, with several other officers from 2 Commando, being taken down all the way to Brindisi for a parachuting course. Even though Jos had overcome his fear of heights in his early commando training, it was another big challenge. But, as usual, he made light of it in his letters:

We fell out of an aeroplane sufficient times to earn our wings . . . We went in a party, and though no-one can ever say they really loved the moments when they were in the plane, it was great fun and a grand experience. One of the blokes (Alec Parsons) had never been up in an aeroplane before - so he has gone up a number of times but has never landed!

Having made his requisite five jumps successfully, he returned to Vis and a considerable shock. In his absence a raid had gone very wrong, and the unthinkable had happened: Jack Churchill had been taken prisoner. He was leading a huge raid on the German-held island of Bra with an improvised force of over a thousand commandos and Partisans. Two garrisons had been successfully stormed, but in attempting a third coup, a night-time assault up a heavily fortified hill, they were met with formidable resistance. 'Mad Jack', to inspire his men, had playing the liveliest of tunes on his bagpipes as he led the attack, but enemy fire was overwhelming and eventually only he and five others (most of them seriously wounded) managed to reach the summit. Suddenly, echoing down to the valley below came a sound no-one had heard their commander play before, the plaintive *Will Ye No Come Back Again?* It was the final statement. As he fought off a charge of some twenty Germans single-handedly, Churchill was knocked temporarily unconscious by a grenade. In this most ill-fated of raids, 80 commandos were killed and over 300 wounded before the operation was aborted. With the capture of the C.O., Jos was now one of only three officers who had originally sailed with the unit from Scotland to Gibraltar.

The legend of 'Mad Jack', however, was not scotched by his capture. Rather, indeed, it was augmented. Erroneously thought to be related to Winston Churchill, he was eventually imprisoned near Berlin in Sachsenhausen concentration camp (recently installed with gas chambers and ovens to avoid overcrowding). Ever resourceful, Churchill tunneled his way out, and although eventually recaptured and sent to a high-security camp in the Austrian Tyrol, he utilized a floodlight failure to make good a speedy departure, this time crossing the Alps on foot and walking a further 150 miles before rejoining the Allies in North Italy.

Jos's 24<sup>th</sup> birthday was spent on Vis, and it brought good news, promotion to Captain, which meant he took over the leadership of 5 Troop for a while, when the much admired Dickie Hooper eventually returned home, giving in at last to the several wounds he had gallantly attempted to ignore.

News of the war, too, brought further comfort, particularly in the area which had cost Pat Henderson's life:

The news from Italy is really good tonight - I heard it on the radio from London – I'm glad that the show has started so successfully - it does mean a lot to have captured Cassino and broken the Gustav Line. Just let the armour get cracking and Jerry will be running for his life . . .

Like everyone else, he was full of admiration for the 8<sup>th</sup> Army's leader:

What a great character Monty is - really fascinating. The troops loved him and Mike Webb (who apes his speech and mannerisms - throwing in divisions with a sweep of his arm!) cannot rate him too high. A man you really trust for the almost superhuman task of throwing in a Second Front and maintaining it. "Gentlemen, I read my Bible every morning and I heartily advise you to do too." Yes, say I, England can do with a man like that at this hour - you were born for it - pray God you may use your opportunity to the full.

In addition to the stimulating optimism of Mike Webb, there was also that of a young subaltern, John Barton, whose MC had just been augmented by the DSO for a particularly daring feat in true film star style, for which he acquired the nickname of Errol Flynn. Barton also came from Sussex, so he and Jos were able to reminisce together happily. ("Yesterday, on the hard pebbles by the sea, we talked of Birling Gap, of Fairlight and the pronunciation of Sea-ford!") And on Vis there was a third new friend: "And this time, praise be, a kindred spirit as well – an ordinand!" Major John Wakeling, like Jos, had earlier been very involved in the Cambridge Inter-Collegiate Christian Union. He was later to become a leading churchman.

2 Commando carried on under new leadership, Major Ted Fynn now taking over as Commanding Officer, and for a while they continued causing disruption on Yugoslavia's coast. But eventually, after 5 months in Vis, the Commandos withdrew from the area, mainly at the fiercely nationalistic Partisans' own request. The island was still hugely important strategically, but over-crowded, swamped with Partisans driven out of their Serbian stronghold by the Nazis. Jos had noted a new atmosphere. The Dalmatian marching songs were no longer to be heard. Those who sang them had largely perished. The new Partisans on the island seemed less eccentric and loveable, more sober and committed to their communist ideologies. Tito himself had been spirited out of central Bosnia just in time to evade capture. One of Jos's last memories of Vis was of Tito himself, newly arrived in the island, inspecting 2 Commando:

A flattened vineyard which had been turned into a football pitch was selected for the parade. To the stirring sound of the pipes of the Highland Light Infantry, Tito emerged from an armoured car, surrounded by motor-cyclists with tommy guns. He shook hands with all of our officers, and, after the march past, read a speech in Serbo-Croat which Brigadier Tom Churchill translated for us. It ended with the cry 'Long Live the freedom-loving peoples of the world!'

Jos later commented on the immense amount of preparation for the event – "the spit and polish would have rivalled any parade ground and the only difference was the bristling Tommy guns" – as well as Tito's "bear-like hand grasp" and appearance. Despite "strong features and a very fine face", he looked much older and fatter than in his photographs.

But it was with few regrets that, on 5 July 1944, Jos and 2 Commando said their final goodbyes to Commander Cerni, Komanda Majesta and the various other local representatives lined up on the quay.

As so often happens, politics had come to destroy a magnificent natural affinity between those who were allies by force of circumstance but friends through the comradeship of strife.

There had been one glorious party the night before departure. And the stark little island suddenly showed off all its quaint attractions as Jos surveyed it one final time for his parents' benefit:

The countryside is looking quite green. The grape bushes make even the bare mountain sides look quite flourishing (though it is a continual fight against natural obstacles to produce a yearly crop). Odd patches of corn are stuck into the places with the best soil, with grapes all round it. There are no modern methods of planting, reaping or tilling - just the old hand sowing, scything and spade-ploughing. They are a hardy people who earn every penny they force out of the land.

Soon 2 Commando would be back in Italy, for a two-week break in quarters near Monopoli, on the coast south of Bari, before re-crossing the Adriatic for a new challenge. The commandos' six months in Vis had caused the Nazis trouble and boosted Tito's cause. But now, as Tito assumed control there, all that was left to show for such earnest gallantry was a plaque in the old naval cemetery, juxtaposing the words of A.E. Housman with two lines from the Old Testament in salute of those who had given up their lives in that summer of 1944:

Here dead we lie
because we did not choose
to live and shame the land
from which we sprung.
Life, to be sure,
is nothing much to lose,
but young men think it is
and we were young.

They shall be mine, saith the Lord of Hosts,
In that day when I make up my jewels.

# 20

# DAVID: LOST IN AN ALBACORE

On his return to the *Pretoria Castle* from his leave in London, David had an enthusiastic reception from his Commanding Officer. At last there would be some decent deck-landings again, he was told, after all the imperfections of the past fortnight! David felt understandably flattered. And shortly afterwards, he and his fellow pilots were "showered with congratulations" on a successful test with the unloved Barracuda, simulating faulty landings in which the plane's hook did not catch an arrestor wire centrally and thereby slowed the plane less effectively. He confided to his parents: "Pride's a rotten thing, even if we keep it to ourselves, isn't it?" These 'off-centre' trials, however, were followed by even more spectacular ones in which the aeroplane was 'bounced' before it met the wires. ("As before, this came very naturally, and everyone was delighted.")

There was further excitement when some brand-new American Harvard fighters arrived, the fastest aeroplanes David had yet flown.

They go like the proverbial bomb. I haven't fully explored them yet, because they are just out of their boxes and are still restricted in some respects.

He discovered they were strongly made when he crashed one on landing. ("Not to put too fine a point on it, it was a shaky do.") The work was so intensive it even carried on over Christmas. God, as he later admitted, was beginning to take second place to the Admiralty. Then in February 1944 (while Jos, a thousand miles away, was just beginning his time with the

Partisans on Vis) came the happening which was to shape David's priorities for the rest of his life.

It had seemed just a routine flight, taking a Fairey Albacore from Crail westwards across Scotland to the *Pretoria Castle* in the Clyde. He had no crew, for he was carrying a heavy consignment of radio equipment, crated up and ready to be tried out on the ship. Included amongst it all was the prototype of the radio beacon which was later to be adopted by airlines and air forces all over the world, saving the lives of countless people who came down in the sea. Still later, it was to be fitted to American spacecraft to assist in their recovery from the ocean. But on this particular February day, all the equipment he was ferrying was nothing more to David than just another untried British invention.

An Albacore of David's squadron

He set off in the middle of the afternoon, with the weather reasonable over the east coast but known to be poor further west. He climbed up, edging round the south of Edinburgh, skirting the Forth rail bridge and its balloon barrage, and moving across the south of Glasgow into the valley down which he intended to fly en route to the Clyde and the *Pretoria Castle.*

All had gone well until he turned into the valley. There he found the clouds were well down on the hills to either side, but the valley was a wide one and he would have plenty of room, he thought, to turn round through 180 degrees and come out of it, if the cloud came too low. As he did not have a radio in the Albacore, it was absolutely essential that he stayed below the clouds, and they continued to get lower and lower, forcing him again and again to throttle back and descend, to stay in visual contact with the ground. Eventually, when the outline of the fields in the valley below again became hazy and he throttled back, the haze failed to vanish. This decided him that the cloud was too low for comfort and he must return the way he had come, turning round through 180 degrees, a basic manoeuvre on which, in cloud, he depended on his gyro-controlled direction indicator. He was not as yet unduly perturbed. But as he gently started the turn, he was shocked to see that his gyro indicator, instead of showing him the direction in which he was pointing, was spinning round helplessly. Suddenly he was flying blind, no longer sure of the proximity of the surrounding mountains. And so he returned, as best he could, to his original direction, flying down what he hoped was still the valley.

The most urgent course of action was to try to get himself above the height of the mountains. This would mean turning and climbing. He was not very happy at having to climb up through so much cloud, but he began the process, furious with himself for having got into such a situation. For the first thousand feet the climb went smoothly, despite the Albacore being a cumbersome aircraft at the best of times and currently extra-heavily laden. Only if there were an icing level in the cloud, would he be in serious trouble . . .

I began to feel extremely lonely and would have given anything at this point for a radio. The only comfort was that I had no crew to worry about, and if I could get sufficient height, I might be able to bale out.

At this stage, however, he became conscious of another worrying factor: he was having difficulty in controlling his speed, which was tending to drop away from his safe climbing speed of 90 knots. He accordingly eased the control column forward. A glance outside the cockpit confirmed his worst fears. There was a shiny film of ice forming on the leading edge of the wings. For the first time, he felt really fearful:

I thought again of baling out. But I had insufficient height to do so and, anyway, I was too frightened and angry with myself to make the attempt.

So he concentrated on another, final attempt to force the aircraft to climb.

With the control column eased forward, the speed built up rapidly to 90 again, but I could not hold it there. Up it went: 95, 100, 110, 120. I was obviously beginning to dive but now the effect of the control column being eased backwards was beginning to tell and the speed was dropping again. I tried to anticipate, to stop it at 90, but it fell away rapidly past that figure. Back the needle swung: 80, 70 - there was a shudder and I had obviously stalled. Control column right forward, full throttle - the needle began to creep up again: 120, 130, 140. The altimeter was dropping too: I must be near to the level of the valley. Nothing I could do seemed to prevent this awful loss of height.

For the next few nightmare minutes David continued the struggle, but it was one he no longer felt capable of winning. Somehow he had to find the necessary speed, to gain height and keep turning; and somehow, too, he had to keep control of himself. He knew that if he lost control of co-ordination of mind, hands and feet, he was finished. At one moment, when he took his eyes off the instruments for a second and looked out of the cockpit, he saw the slate roofs of a row of houses, wet and glistening in the rain. At another moment, he had a glimpse of the mountainside, rocks and tufts of grass, as he pulled away in a blistering turn back into the cloud. He hung onto the controls, the stick, the throttle, the rudder, in a final agonising attempt to master the situation. He knew that he must hit something soon. His physical control was failing. He was almost blinded by sweat and feeling terribly sick.

What happened next, at this very critical moment, was something he was to write down in later life with great care:

Suddenly, above the noise of the engine and the slipstream, I heard, with indescribable clearness, "Let go, David, let go". And there was light in the cockpit which, like the words, seemed to come from behind my right shoulder. I remember looking round, behind my shoulder, to see where the voice and the radiant light was coming from. But all I saw was the great petrol tank which fitted the rear of the cockpit. It had been an absolute command to do the one thing I was utterly afraid of doing. My hands, my feet, my eyes, my reactions were all that stood between me and the aeroplane going into a stall. But there it was, as clearly as any words I had ever heard spoken, "Let go, David, let go". And I did, instantly. Hands off the controls, feet off the rudder, eyes off the instruments. The voice came again: "Set your gyro. Fly straight." I set the gyro, put my feet and hands back on the controls and kept the number steady on the direction instrument. "Now climb," the voice said. It was still clear, but much quieter. Strangely, now I had no difficulty at all in achieving a steady climbing speed, but all the time I had not been prepared to fly straight at any cost because, to do so at that height meant that the chances must be overwhelming that I would hit a mountain.

No longer worrying that this might happen, David climbed and climbed until he came out into glorious sunshine at about 8,000 feet.

Never had the sun, clear blue sky and the white carpet of cloud below looked so good! It was wonderful and I viewed with complete calm the fact that there was a thick layer of cloud covering the whole of the area within my flight range; that I had no idea where the upper winds were or where I was now situated relative to the ground; and that I had no radio. I was feeling contented and happy - totally unaffected by the very serious danger of my circumstances. I was waiting for instructions and they came to me as a kind of quiet, still, small voice: I was to fly to the east, descend over the North Sea and return to my base.

So David flew eastward for about three-quarters of an hour. He was almost certain that he must be well over the North Sea by now - indeed, if the winds were westerly, he thought he might already be out of range of land and have to ditch. Had he been flying completely by himself, he would have descended in an attempt to locate dry land. Instead, he carried on exactly as he was, and kept listening, open to instructions.

And, sure enough, it came to me with quiet conviction that I should continue flying easterly for a further ten minutes, and only then descend.

David did so. And, as he finally descended and came through the cloud, he felt curiously unafraid. There, suddenly, was the sea beneath him. But there, too, not all that far away, was land! He turned towards it and recognised with gratitude the familiar outline of St Abb's Head. One look at the cloud-covered mountains behind, over which he had just passed, made him very grateful indeed for the last ten minutes of easterly flying.

David pointed the Albacore north towards Fifeness, and, ten minutes later, landed safely at Crail.

# 21
# JOS: TWO SORTIES IN ALBANIA

2 Commando returned to south Italy, to a large base on the Apulian coast a few miles north of Molfetta. They were there only two weeks before their next assignment, just long enough for Jos to tidy up: "The wretched barber reeked of garlic! Horrible! But these Italians are first-class at the hair-cutting racket!" He was also able to catch up with paper work which included some very difficult letters as he was now the unit's secretary for the Next-of-Kin Assistance Committee. The glorious Italian sunshine made two outdoor Church Parades memorable occasions - "The singing is such fun in an olive grove" - and perhaps encouraged Jos to concede that Padre Gareth Banting "gave his best sermon to date".

2 Commando's new target was again up the east coast of the Adriatic, only this time in Albania. Their mission: a 24-hour, lightning raid against the German coastal garrison at Spilje, which, if knocked out, would open up the Adriatic coastline to the Albanian partisans (who were now gallantly harassing their conquerors), enabling the Allies to provide them with much-needed stores and munitions. In the aftermath of Vis, 2 Commando's numbers were down to 250, and Jos was the Acting Adjutant in the raid, the right-hand-man to the Commanding Officer, Ted Fynn.

This first-ever British operation in Albania was far from straightforward. After landing before midnight near Spilje, they had an approach march of four miles amid wild mountains. Their objective, a high ridge overlooking the village of Himare, was very strongly fortified by the Germans. Any surprise they had hoped to achieve for their dawn attack was wrecked by the anxious barking of dogs in the village, each outbreak arousing random machine-gun fire from the Germans at the top of the ridge. At dawn, Ted Fynn's commandos began their assault up the steep slopes:

The German defenders had established excellent fields of fire. Progress by the Commando was slow as many barbed-wire obstacles were encountered and anti-personnel 'S' mines seemed to be going off all over the hillside. After 10.00 a.m. about 100 of the enemy had been knocked out by the Commandos. Col. Ted Fynn ordered a withdrawal as a strict time-limit had been laid in the operation orders. So No. 2 disengaged and returned to the embarkation point. (Bob Bishop: *Operations in Albania*)

The raid had been planned in careful conjunction with the partisans, and though, on the commandos' withdrawal, some 40 Germans had been left on the ridge, an entire partisan brigade subsequently attacked and eliminated them. The objective of the Spilje raid, the enabling of supplies being shipped in from Italy, was therefore achieved. But with twenty killed and over sixty wounded, 2 Commando was now down to half strength.

2 Commando on their 24-hour raid at Spilje

Attacking the ridge over Himare

A commando searches a captured German - an Albanian partisan looks on

A wounded commando is carried back from the attack on the Spilje garrison

So, back on the Apulian coast above Molfetta, there was a further period of recruitment and regrouping, a taxing time for Jos as Acting Adjutant. Conditions were quite good. They lived in tents, sleeping on stretchers rather than palliases, but having mosquito nets and the use of a wooden hut as a Mess. Jos was allocated his own jeep, and one of his recruitment drives took him across Italy on dusty roads to Naples. He was busy, too, driving to local towns to visit the wounded in hospitals, which were often alarmingly dirty and ill-equipped.

Then came a real blessing, a chance encounter with a former Cambridge friend in Italy on War Office business, who introduced him to a thriving church in nearby Barletta, where a vigorous Methodist minister was leading large, ever-changing congregations of widely different denominations. Thanks to his jeep, Jos was able to motor over to the church most Sunday mornings and evenings, when there would usually be 150-200 servicemen present, and he sometimes joined the Sunday afternoon tea party at the manse, where they had singing round a harmonium from the Wesleyan

Hymn Book. ("Oh what memories!" wrote Jos of the first occasion. "I chose 'Oh Safe To The Rock' and we had bags of old favourites!") After his many disappointments, there was real joy at "the first Gospel sermon" he had heard for over a year:

In the morning it was *Isaiah* 43. And, oh, how I thought back over the past 12 months when he read verses 2 and 3. And so to verse 10: 'Ye are my witnesses'. What a privilege and responsibility. In the evening it was Genesis 19.11 (last phrase) and John 10.9. A text taken out of its context - and quite legitimately so in my opinion. People like Humphrey Playford used to consider that an automatic condemnation of a speaker!

Over the coming months the Barletta Free Church's fellowship was to bring him much joy and encouragement.

Jos had been away from England for well over a year by now, and a ten-day leave in August was extremely welcome. He and a couple of fellow officers decided to visit Rome, which had only been liberated that summer, and Salerno. They headed off, by chance, on the first anniversary of the fighting at Scarletta in Sicily and the death of John Jeffreys. ("It seems so much longer ago and I can barely bring his sunny character back to memory. What a price, it is!") Transport was a problem but they managed to cadge a flight on an army plane:

We stopped for half-an-hour at Naples, ran over the old Anzio bridgehead and then circled the city. It was a terrific sight and I managed to pick out the Coliseum and St Peter's while we were coming in.

Their hotel was "dark and gloomy", its residents inclined to keep themselves to themselves. The forbiddingly silent atmosphere in the city was hardly surprising. It was only a year since the Nazis had taken it over. Since then over Allied 100,000 sorties had bombed strategic targets - and bombing at that period was a notoriously imprecise business - with the loss of 600 aircraft. 60,000 tons of bombs had been dropped just in the two months preceding its capture. "The glory that was Rome," commented Jos sadly, "is no glory now." Nonetheless, he was able to visit several of the famous tourist sites, sometimes on foot, sometimes by jeep, St Peter's predictably eliciting a mixed response:

Peter and Paul are worshipped at the expense of Christ. It struck us all very forcibly that with all the statues and mosaics that clutter St Peter's, Christ appears but twice - once on the Cross and once in the Transfiguration. (The latter is a lovely painting by Raphael with the Demoniac child in the foreground and the disciples unable to help him, but just pointing to where He is.)

After Rome they travelled south to Cassino, where savage fighting had lasted for four months earlier that year. 1,400 tons of bombs had been dropped on the little hill-town and its ruins were awesome:

What an education Cassino was. If they want a permanent war memorial to illustrate the foolishness of Mussolini, there it is, in all its tragedy. And if, after all, someone should ask, 'Is it worth it?', there is the answer. No man-made monument could compare in sheer tragic beauty to the shambles that was Cassino . . .

From Cassino they travelled, via Naples and Pompeii, to Salerno.

It was just 11 months since I'd been there last. It all looked strange and very peaceful. I went to see the cemetery where all the Commando graves now are, but found that some had not yet been named, so couldn't find Frank Mason's or Morny's.

Seeing it again, at this length of time, made me realise that Salerno itself and the peninsula with Sorrento, Ravello, Amalfi and Maiori, are the most beautiful spots in Italy.

They hitch-hiked back to Barletta, arriving just in time for a Church Parade celebrating a National Day of Prayer. Disappointed that the Padre had not risen to the occasion ("I fear he was 'punch-less' - what a glorious opportunity for praise for the past and hope for the future, all in His Hands!"), Jos repaired to Barletta and more vigorous fare:

Tea at the Manse and then we went out for the Open Air service. What an experience! On the sea front, not far from a large NAAFI. I had to get up on my feet. Oh that God may have used my lips to all those soldiers and perhaps to some of the Italians there. And then back for the 7.00 o'clock service in the church where a naval padre gave a grand word on 'But whom think ye" with some really glorious hymns, including 'And Can It Be.' Really well sung. Oh how I praise him for having brought me to this place.

This fellowship was all the more important to Jos when he received the news of the death in action of a close friend from his Cambridge days, Donald Creaton, who had been fighting in France since the D-Day landings that June. Jos had received a most moving letter from Donald's mother, thanking him for his prayers:

Donald was killed instantly while on patrol. God was very merciful to take him like that. They buried him by the Calvary in the little village where it happened, and the village people covered his grave with flowers. I like to think that he lies beside the Cross and where people have prayed for generations. But I know he would not want us to dwell on thoughts of his grave, so I keep trying to think of him as more alive than ever he was, and serving his Master in complete joy. I think he understands now why this had to happen, and how God's will is best and right for us all . . .

It has been a real strength and comfort to me to have had so many letters from all sorts of people saying what a help and inspiration his life had been to them, and how from knowing Donald they were drawn closer to Christ . . .

Jos struggled to come to terms with the loss of such a dear friend, telling his parents:

I still can't believe somehow that I'll never see him till we meet 'up there' and Cambridge would seem to be impossible without the thought of him being round the corner or quietly walking in to drag me off to the Saturday evening prayer meeting. Oh God, we are paying for this war - and what a cost. How often we plead, "Why take the best?' Why shouldn't it have been someone else? - why not me? - rather than Donald? Yes, may I say reverently, 'God make me worthier, make me stronger to follow where Donald has led the way.' Please pray that I may realise (I can't at the moment) that his passing is something to praise God for . . .

Amid all the tragedy of war, the boisterous spirit of the Commandos must have been wonderfully uplifting. There were two particularly high-spirited celebrations that September, the first marking the promotion of the unit's popular Rhodesian commander, Ted Fynn, from Major to Lieutenant-Colonel. It was held at the picturesque Grotto at Polignano, a little town not only built dramatically on top of precipitous cliffs, but also inside them, the caves of Polignano leading to glorious terraces with startlingly rich views of the blue and silver Adriatic.

Taking over a Commando unit from someone as charismatic as Jack Churchill would have been a hard job, but Fynn had brought it off successfully. He was an intelligent man, and it was while at university that he had come, like David, under the influence of the Oxford Group. "It is a great advantage to have a C.O. who is interested in religion," Jos had commented at the time of his appointment, while regretting that perhaps he had lost his way a little and had "decided views of his own".

The second celebration, held in Bari itself, was for Fynn's marriage to an officer in the Field Ambulance Nursing Yeomanry - a cover for the Special Services. (Fynn's bride was probably not nursing at all but listening in to German broadcasts to help pin down their latest army positions.) The wedding, at Bari's Protestant Church, St Augustine's, was taken by Padre Gareth Banting, with Jos and his fellow officers acting as ushers, and afterwards Fynn's officers formed an unusual Guard of Honour outside the church using their commando fighting knives instead of the more traditional swords. George 'Alec' Parsons, who had been the unit's most inventive joker since joining 2 Commando in Gibraltar, somehow managed to do terrible things to the jeep to which Fynn now carried his bride, to drive her to the reception. First, there was a big (but harmless) bang when they sat on the seat. Next, another bang as Fynn touched the starter motor. There were six bangs in all, by which time they discovered they had no engine. (Alec Parsons had had it removed.) Amid great laughter, one team of sergeants fired Very pistols and mortar flares and another laid a smokescreen, while a piper piped a joyful farewell - the signal for eight brawny commandos to begin pushing the happy couple off in the engine-less jeep. Away they went, tin cans clattering over Bari's bumpy, paved streets, as the couple were propelled at great speed to a suitably boisterous wedding party.

The Fynns arrived back from their honeymoon shortly before a major mission, a return to Albania, also involving several other units - notably 9 Commando and 43 Royal Marine Commando. They set out on 22 September 1944, believing they were on a 50-hour operation in and around the German-held port of Sarande. Once a popular holiday resort known as 'the Pearl of the Albanian Riviera', Sarande was strategically important, situated on the mainland just a mile from the island of Corfu (still heavily garrisoned by the Nazis) and an obvious evacuation port for the Germans' planned withdrawal from Greece. The commandos were to land six miles to the north of the city, carry out demolitions on the Sarande-Delvine road and generally harass the Sarande garrison as best they could, before effecting a speedy withdrawal.

This plan, however, was over-ridden, at the very last possible moment, by a new and very bureaucratic planning organization which had suddenly become very powerful. Called Land Forces Adriatic (and soon known by 2 Commando as 'Lunatic Farces Idiotic'), it was based, for some strange reason, in Cairo. Just as the Commando units were setting out, the L.F.A. decreed that Sarande should be subject to a full Brigade attack, with the Commandos at its centre. Instead of doing what damage they could to Sarande on a hit-and-run operation, they were now to spearhead the capture of the city, garrisoned by 2,000 Germans and defended by a whole range of concreted artillery positions and bren gun emplacements, so very well entrenched that many of them still survive over sixty years on. It was not much of a battle plan.

2 Commando sailed from Italy in summer weather, wearing light combat dress suitable for the 50-hour raid, and, having landed at midnight on Sugar Beach, found that the valley down which they had been told to advance was impassable, defended by at least 20 artillery positions. To proceed down it would simply mean immediate annihilation. So back in Cairo, they hit upon an alternative. The commandos should change direction, cross a large mountain range, and then make good their attack. Even in fine weather, with proper equipment, this would have been a massive challenge:

The mountains rose to 2,000 feet, thickly wooded on the lower slopes but with rocky crags, which in places had innumerable pointed rock-projections, about 9 inches high and 6 inches apart ( a sort of miniature Giant's Causeway), which made walking both painful and dangerous.

And no sooner were they there than "with terrifying suddenness" it began to rain. An eight-day non-stop deluge ensued.

Lying asleep the first night in a 2-man bivouac with the Colonel, I was awoken at 2 o'clock by a noise like a mighty waterfall. Suddenly the dry bed of a stream beside which we had pitched our tent became a racing tide. All our kit, including blankets, were washed away. We grabbed what we could and made for higher ground. For the remaining hours till dawn we shivered under a tiny shrub. It was impossible to light a fire – all the matches were soaked. It was the same for everyone. There was no shelter and nowhere to get dry and cook a meal. Progress was impossible. It was a question of sheer survival. But by the end of the second day on the mountain we had almost run out of emergency self-heating soups.

The attack was put off on all fronts for the rain to stop - and it took 8 days, by which time 2 Commando had only a third of its men fit to fight, such were the effects of exposure, exhaustion and, in particular, the ravages of trench foot. One night was spent in a desperate attempt to use the shelter of a tumbledown monastery:

Its only room had a gaping hole in the roof. A vast fire was built in the middle and everyone stripped down and hung his wet clothes and blankets in front of the fire. Guards were mounted, not to watch for the enemy but to see that the fire was kept burning and that none of the clothes caught light. Some did a voluntary stint on guard while the bitterly cold wind froze them as they stood naked until their clothes dried. The rain poured down the hole threatening to put the fire out. Others meanwhile lay down on the stone-slabbed floor, trying to sleep. Yet within 48 hours of this, the Commando was made ready to take its part in the attack.

Their attack, with fixed bayonets, went in at dawn and by 11.30 2 Commando had overrun their two objectives, gun positions defending the town. But Alec Parsons, smiling to the last and leading his Troop with immense courage, had perished under withering German machine-gun fire. Losses were heavy, but, with 40 Commando leading, they now succeeded in forcing their way into the town. By 4.30 the last of the street fighting was over, and Sarande was captured.

That evening, Padre Gareth Banting went back to the scene of the unit's attack to bury those who had died. He performed a simple ceremony and was turning back to throw some more earth on the graves, when there was a sudden explosion and a cry. He had walked onto a hidden minefield. A fellow officer lifted him up, applied a tourniquet and tried to carry him down, but he had no medical equipment with him and by the time he reached their jeep the Padre had died. It had been a bitter three-week operation in unbelievably wretched conditions. Equipped for a 50-hour operation, the commandos had to wear the same clothes and boots, day in day out. There was no opportunity for washing or shaving. But, having gained the town, they could have experienced an even more bitter aftermath, for the Germans had booby-trapped its centre.

Fortunately our remarkable Brigade Engineer prevented even greater carnage. Finding an empty case which had contained safety fuses, he deduced that a high explosive charge must be buried under the concrete floor of some shops. The Brigadier ordered the centre of the town to be roped off and 48 hours after its surrender the whole of the main square blew up. Although wounded in the explosion, the Engineer continued to work and reported that another charge would go off the next day. This time the whole town was evacuated. The explosion, when it came, was even bigger than the first.

The Brigade attack had included Corfu, which surrendered the next day, Ted Fynn taking three Troops over to the island to clear up any surviving pockets of resistance. The Greeks were very welcoming, and even put on a game of cricket. It was the final bizarre event in an extraordinary mission.

2 Commando departing from the beach at Sarande

For Jos's family in Sussex there had been two worrying weeks of silence. Then, on October 3, came a short note, scribbled in pencil, wishing his father a happy birthday. ("I do hope you haven't been worried. We are all fit and well, though a trifle damp.") Then after a further ten days' silence, a letter arrived in which Jos gave little away, though he did allow himself a sombre generalization:

It will be impossible to talk about it afterwards, what we have been through in the past 3 weeks, for people will only think we have been exaggerating ...

And the Sarande tragedies weighed so heavily with him that finally he gave some details:

As always, it has meant the loss of some of the very best. Alec Parsons was a great soul and a first-class Troop Commander. The very soul of cheerfulness under the worst possible conditions and a great inspiration to his men – an ideal Commando officer. He caught it – and so did Jim Coyle and our Padre. Only in their death do you realize something of what they meant to you. How one wishes one could have been of more use to them in their lives. The Padre was one of the type that English gentlemen are made of. He knew all about Evangelical teaching, he was sincere, but he couldn't accept our way.

A day later, in the immediate wake of the Sarende tragedies, Jos had some encouraging news:

I had a grand chat with the Colonel last night. He had seen me bungling my kit together earlier on and had noticed my copy of *Practical Christianity*. He immediately pounced on it, read the Prayer of an American Midshipman and asked if he could keep it. In the evening he asked me how you joined the Officers' Christian Union and asked various questions about it. Oh, how I praised Him who doeth all things well and prayed for strength and guidance. The Colonel has often shown an interest in religious things and was very keen to hear that I was a possible ordinand. He felt the Padre's death very much. He took the burial service himself and read it very well. I know that you will pray that he may be brought to know more than the mere superficial covering that goes for Christianity, that he may be brought into personal contact with his Saviour. I am getting the O.C.U. application form off straight away.

# 22

# DAVID ON THE PRETORIA CASTLE

At the time when Jos had been helping Tito's partisans, in the late Spring of 1944, David had applied to the Admiralty for a transfer from the Service Trials Unit back to active combat. It was shortly before D-Day, and there was much talk about the possibility of an attempted liberation of France. He had explained to his parents:

It's not that I am brave. In fact, it's partly to convince myself that I'm not a complete coward. I'm sure you'll understand my attitude when one thinks what a critical moment in history this is. I'm not sure that I'll be able to get out of this wizard job, but I was told today that I may be successful. I can't be quite content continuing with these trials when so much is going on. Please pray that I may be led to the right job or kept here, according to His will . . .

The request was eventually turned down, and David returned to Crail, cheerfully disguising any disappointment he may have felt:

That their Lordships feel able to do without my direct assistance in the assault on Europe is an astonishing fact. You couldn't ask for better evidence of the confidence they feel about the outcome of the present operation!

There were many compensations for the frustration of not being able to participate in the crucial battle for Europe, and David was very alive to them:

The scenery today was even more lovely than I've ever seen in Scotland before - and that's saying something! The colourings of the mountains, the light and shade of cloud, was really affecting. One way, I came by Stirling Valley. It was glorious. Made you want to sing and cry at the same time!

There was also an interesting diversification in the work when he spent several months doing acceptance trials on three aircraft-carriers, the *Indomitable* and the newly-built *Indefatigable* and *Implacable*:

What we do is to go with the various types that the ship will later operate and do a few landings and take-offs. This tests the arrestor gear for tension at different weights and speeds. Each ship is different to some extent and has different currents which may affect aircraft as they get near the stern or leave the bows. The latter particularly affect cross-wind catapult launches.

He of course omitted to tell his parents that he himself was leading a charmed life in a job which continued to be extremely hazardous.

David emerges unscathed from a Seafire after crashing into the *Pretoria Castle* barrier, March 1945

That autumn two of the newest members of his squadron, whom he had been training up for operational carrier work, flew into a hillside during a snowstorm. In another tragic accident, two top scientists, flying with David's squadron, were killed. The stress was continual and severe. When a dear friend of his went missing, he spent a fruitless two and a half hours leading the search. He himself had (at the very least) eight serious incidents in this period. He crash-landed an ailing Barracuda at Ayr. A Swordfish ended up nose first in the *Pretoria Castle's* deck, and an Albacore with a smashed tail.

A Firefly only inches from total disaster

When the hook snapped on a Barracuda, he again crashed into the ship's safety barrier, and the same barrier saved him twice when he was testing the Fairey Firefly (a new fighter fitted with the very latest American radar), the accelerator leg jamming on one occasion, and the undercarriage failing (at night) on another. Twice, too, the barriers prevented him plunging into the sea in a recalcitrant Seafire, a version of the Spitfire being developed (with enormous difficulty) for carrier use.

The Seafire's initial accident record was appalling, for Spitfires were designed for long runways, and their landing speed and the steepness of their angle of descent added extra problems to what was, even in the best of conditions, a hazardous operation. (In the whole of the war more carrier aircraft were lost to accidents than combat with the enemy.) The Seafire first saw major action at Salerno, in support of Operation Avalanche, when over a third of the 120 used there were destroyed in carrier-related accidents. In addition to the problems of their sheer speed, other faults included poor visibility from the cockpit, a short and weak undercarriage and an alarming tendency to 'peck' on landing, which resulted in the propeller touching the deck. But such was the Seafire's outstanding performance in aerial combat that the Navy persevered in its development and, in the end, it proved one of the Trials Unit's greatest successes. An aviation historian recently wrote:

Another of David's own lucky escapes—a 'prang' in a Fairey Swordfish,
August 1944

In the closing weeks of the war the Seafire eventually proved itself a capable carrier aircraft. When properly equipped and operated by well-trained pilots and maintenance personnel, it finally gained a respectability undreamed of when it first appeared on a carrier deck. (Donald Nijboer, *Aeroplane*, August 2010)

The Firefly caused almost as many problems, and even when it was passed for service, David remained extremely anxious about one particular aspect. He took it upon himself, therefore, to write to the squadron which was receiving the newly modified aircraft, just in case his official report was held up. It was. And a grateful Squadron Commander replied: "If you had not written to us, then probably we would not have received the official version until we had all killed ourselves."

A Grumann Avenger after a less than perfect landing

Whatever his inner regret at not being able to be involved in the historic final push to rid Europe of the Nazis, David was fascinated by all the varied new challenges of his job and remained hugely grateful for it. And ever since that afternoon in February, when he had been lost in the Scottish clouds in a radio-less Albecore, he was quietly and humbly convinced that God had work for him to do. Quite what it would be, he had no idea. It was all a question of keeping listening.

# 23

# JOS: THREE LAST BATTLES IN ITALY

For 2 Commando, the serious losses suffered in Albania led to a 4-month period of recruitment and training (from October 1944 to mid-February 1945), spent at the same base (north of Molfetta on the Apulian coast) from which they had set out for Sarande. Jos was again at the heart of this process, which involved much travel by jeep, including one challenging trip to the west coast. ("We had a shocking journey over to Naples, and, believe it or not, went through a pukka snowstorm!") While at Naples he found time to think of fallen comrades (something he was to do for the rest of his life), but this visit to the battlefields around Dragonea and Piegolelle proved strangely disorientating, for the countryside had been seriously affected by the huge lava flow from the eruption of Vesuvius in March 1944, even to the extent of filling in trenches. ("It was hard to realise we were in the same place.")

This lengthy stay in the Molfetta-Barletta area allowed Jos more time with the Barletta Free Church and its invigorating mix of many nationalities and denominations. Granted a week's leave, he opted to stay at a local Officers' Club and create his own "Convention Week dedicated to the praise of God". It proved a very refreshing time. He was able to attend a series of Free Church evening meetings, and to lead a Bible Study on the Saturday night. ("It was, marvellously enough, 2 Timothy 2 that had just been reached.") Two "glorious" days were spent "in Christian company with picnics in the fields and visits to local grottoes and beauty spots".

Jos, with temporary moustache, after promotion to Captain

The picnics were no doubt all the more glorious for the company of three Christian nurses from South Africa, whom Jos quickly dubbed his three "angels". One of these, Olive, a modest and personable blonde, had attracted his attention early on by her skilful playing of the harmonium at Sunday tea parties at the manse. It was not long before Jos, encouraged perhaps by Colonel Ted Fynn's whirlwind romance earlier in the year, even began to mention in his letters home the possibility of marriage, though he was unsure about the difference in age - Olive was several years the elder - and backgrounds. "We just want to know each other better before we decide on anything," he assured his parents. Perhaps it was these joyful preoccupations which caused him, that November, the embarrassment of mislaying his jeep. ("I've been a naughty boy, and tomorrow morning I'm up before the beak - the Brigadier - for losing my jeep. Oh, the ignominy and shame!")

Jos with (just possibly) two of his 'angels' from the Barletta Free Church

As Christmas approached, he was still in a quandary over Olive, and only too aware that he had not sought God's guidance carefully enough. That December, he reminded himself:

God guides through circumstances, through emotions and through logical thought - and only when I get to an end of Self can I get to the beginning of God - and his plan for me and us.

The Free Church's open-air afternoon services on Sunday afternoons could often be lively, for there was a nearby Naafi which helped swell the numbers clustering around. One Sunday there were loud shouts of "Why don't you win the war with Hitler first?", but when the hecklers came back the next week, Jos was ready for them:

I gave them the illustration of a Troop train waiting in Brighton Station - crowded out - everyone wanting to get to Victoria - and some soldiers getting out and pushing, trying to win the war on their own, while there was an engine in front, with steam and power in the boilers, an engine driver in command, only waiting to put that power into motion. And how, if we're to win the victory that really matters, we need this tremendous POWER in our own lives . . .

Another new activity was a small Bible Study class, which, most encouragingly, involved Colonel Ted Fynn, who had been much moved by the magazine he had borrowed from Jos in Albania. A few weeks after Sarande, Jos had gently suggested to Fynn the start of a Bible Study group. A new Padre would be arriving in days, replied the Colonel, but he'd much prefer Jos (or Joe, as he knew him), to start the class. "And if the Padre doesn't come - in fact, I'd prefer it. But I want to come along myself - and let's call it Joe's Joint"

A few days later, Jos was writing home to say that 'Joe's Joint' duly opened at 6.0 o'clock in Ted Fynn's quarters:

There were four of us (3 couldn't turn up for one reason or another), 2 Privates, the C.O. and myself. I took John 3 with its Necessity of the New Life . . . The discussion afterwards was simply glorious - all the possibilities of the New Life were discussed . . . I know you will pray for this with all its tremendous possibilities - and what a start! Our new Adjutant has asked to come along on Tuesday. Oh for the ability to proclaim the Gospel in all its Truth and Simplicity!

Numbers remained small, but the new Adjutant became a regular attender, and on one occasion the Colonel's new wife, shortly to return home, participated. Two weeks later, mid-December, there was further encouragement, when the Colonel led the group. ("He talked about the first 10 verses of Ephesians 2 and left just the right openings for me to go in and hit"). Soon afterwards, he asked Jos "very humbly and personally" to pray that his wife, who had been put off religion when she was young, might be brought back, not by force or persuasion, but by seeing the extra dimension it was giving his own life.

On the final day of 1944, heavy snowfalls did not prevent Jos from taking to the roads to Barletta:

After a grand service in the morning - and another in the evening taken by a New Zealand Padre, we had the usual Epilogue (consisting of choruses and hymns followed by a short word - this time by a South African lance-corporal who was being repatriated after 3 years abroad). Then there was nothing to do till the Watch Night service at 11.30, so we had some more hymns! Whatever may happen in 1945 it started off magnificently. Just after the minute's silent prayer at midnight, we sang 'Now thank we all our God'. It was simply marvellous.

In the New Year the training intensified, Achnacarry-style, as the commandos readied themselves for further action, but Jos was still able to slip away once a week to Barletta. His letters home were dominated by these Sunday excursions:

—How full of praise I should be at this moment for the marvellous fellowship I'm enjoying . . . The standard of evangelical witness and learning is so very high. The officers (there were 8 at a most intense and glorious Bible Study last night) are from every sort of unit, from every sort of church, and with one glorious common denominator - all one in Christ Jesus. There are sergeants and corporals and privates with whom you feel immediately at home - they are all so gloriously keen.

—Many have been the occasions when getting back into my Jeep after a glorious day I have sung and shouted for joy.

—I had a grand meeting last night in the Free Church House. It was a Fellowship meeting and after prayer all sorts of people just said a word or two - on experiences they had had, on their conversion, on contacts with local Italian Christians, on other meetings going on in different parts of the country. All with a grand feeling of unity, despite the man-made barriers of status or creed. I chose that hymn which has meant so much to me just recently, 'We Rest on Thee, Our Shield and Our Defender' . . . It sounded first-rate . . . Here was the answer, put most simply, to a lot of things I had been thinking about. We Rest on Thee and in Thy Name we go . . .

—It's been a simply marvellous time with Olive. We had a grand time on Sunday evening. The new Free Church padre - a Rev. Grayson - spoke very well on the Christian life as a voyage at sea with the Chart, the Compass (conscience) and the Pilot. Then a wizard after-meeting in the flat. It was just as crowded as ever, though lots seem to have moved on. We used *Golden Bells* - what a joy that is and oh what memories of the seaside and reunions and camp . . .
    I was asked to speak, so said a few words on Joshua. 'Art thou for us or for our adversaries?' . . . 'Nay, but as Captain of the host of the Lord.' Then we had a chorus (which Olive plays so wizardly). 'There's a Name all Names Excelling' . . . Then a closing prayer by a New Zealand Padre who has really been in the thick of it at Cassino and elsewhere, whose prayers are the most natural thing in the world . . .

These precious meetings were clearly drawing to an end, as the fully regrouped 2 Commando, its numbers eventually peaking at an all-time high of 385, spent more and more time on training manoeuvres, day and night. In mid-February they finally left Apulia to move to the north of Italy, where German resistance was still stubborn. It was a big wrench to leave his friends in the fellowship, particularly his three 'angels', whose return to South Africa was now imminent. He and Olive clearly parted on the very best of terms, though they would now seem to have discounted any possibility of marriage:

I could never have imagined that a friendship could have existed on so glorious a basis out in an area like this. Every letter (and she has sweetly promised to write often) which I get will be a reminder of a perfectly gorgeous time or, if necessary, a pinprick to stir me out of lethargy, depression or blackness . . .

A grim rail journey of three and a half days followed. The weather was freezing, and they were travelling in converted cattle-trucks with no heating and with only straw on the floor to offer any comfort, day or night. A single day's rations consisted merely of half a tin of canned meat and a bowl of vegetable soup. But their discomforts were put into perspective by the large number of desperate Italians clinging to the sides of the carriage-trucks, the rooftops and even the couplings between the carriages – a token of the social chaos left in the wake of the fighting. Some jumped off at the brief halts at Caserta or Cassino, where Jos was greeted by further searing images of war:

The sun was just about to go down behind Monte Cassino and the cross on the top which had been untouched throughout the whole battle stood out in silhouette. The shadows were just creeping down on the town as it nestled in the foothills, but all the gaunt tragedy of the spot stood out in its nakedness. To say that there are three repairable buildings in the town is to exaggerate. Stones are only left one upon another because they are so close together they couldn't fall down . . .

Later came a stop at Rome and a slow, tortuous journey through the central Apennines to their destination, Rimini, from where they were taken by road to Ravenna.

This important old town, where Julius Caesar had once gathered his forces before crossing the Rubicon, marked the furthest current extent of the Allied advance on the east side of Italy. Three miles north of Ravenna the Allies had just suffered a big reverse and 2 Commando were part of the reinforcements rushed in to contain a problem which might otherwise develop into a major setback. They first took their place in the Allied front line on 21 February, occupying an area known, unpromisingly, as 'Hades', from where they later moved to 'Gin'.

It was not the usual kind of commando job. With a motley collection of Hussars, Lancers and Italians beside them, they seemed to be pawns in a ferocious game of heavy artillery shelling, like throwbacks from the 1st World War, their bayonets constantly at the ready, their regular forays into no-man's land achieving little other than an increase in the casualty rate. They remained there a month, for the duration of the crisis, spending several days at a time in the line, alternating with short periods of recuperation at a nearby base. There was little sense of progress or achievement, but regular tragedy. Jos' diary for 1945 survives, its empty pages laced with laconic reminders of those killed:

Feb. 25: King caught it
Feb 26: Woods, Campbell, Jackson caught it
Feb 27: Higginbotham caught it
Feb 28: Bampton, Imrie Roud caught it
6 March: Poor Barry O'Meara caught it
11 March: Sgt. Smallbone died of wounds

Nelson Smallbone had been Tottenham Hotspur's reserve goalkeeper just before the war. Big things were expected of him:

He was probably the best-liked character of the whole unit. He never bore the slightest grudge; cared for his men with an almost motherly tenderness; and yet was as cool-headed in action as the fiercest martinet, and with a rather greater sense of responsibility.

Jos' very terse diary entries give occasional hints of what it meant to be in the line for days at a time. On noting the date of the beginning of one rest period, for example, he had commented, "a grand shower". On another occasion: "Out by 12.00. Showers at 1600." Rest periods sometimes involved luxuries like watching *The Way Ahead* at a camp cinema. ("Old Stoic David Niven keeping the flag flying!")

His short, hasty notes home highlighted the determination to keep his spiritual life alive: "Hope to get in a Communion service tomorrow, if I can manage nothing more." "*The Daily Light* of last night was a great help to me." "Olive has been sending a grand supply of helpful pamphlets and booklets."

Amid the grimness of war and the relentless tensions were the occasional lighter moments. One afternoon Ted Fynn suggested to Jos that he should "take a dekko that night" at a suspicious, though seemingly deserted, shack situated in the trees in front of his position. Selecting one of his best snipers to accompany him, Jos duly left his Troop's headquarters, a battered farmhouse, and made a cautious approach:

The moon was very bright, and the land unfortunately dipped away sharply on the enemy side towards a canal along which the Germans were entrenched leaving the two of us very much on the skyline as we made our way between the trees.

Suddenly, the 'phut' of a mortar. Both froze. The bomb landed 20 yards beyond them. As the echo died away there was another 'phut'. This time the crash was about 15 yards the other side. A further rapid series of 'phuts' sent Jos and his lance-corporal diving into the neatest shell-hole, hugging its sides:

Down came the concentration. Each bomb seemed to shake the lip of the crater behind which we were sheltering. When the noise abated, I raised myself, half expecting to see a wave of field-grey uniforms approaching. But there was nothing. So after waiting a seemingly interminable twenty minutes, we moved on. Ahead of us was a derelict German Tiger tank, its gun pointing in our direction. Was it being used as an observation post? Was it booby-trapped?

They approached with caution, and discovered it genuinely derelict. But just as they did so, they heard a noise from behind the shack, now very close. German snipers? Jos edged cautiously towards it, his Colt cocked, "every nerve tingling", and flung open the door dramatically. There was the most glorious of comic anti-climaxes. There were no Nazis in the shack. The noise had come from two hens scratching proudly around their new home.

Later, having returned to the safety of his Headquarters, Jos rang up Ted Flynn. "Just reporting back, sir." "Good show. Was the shack occupied?" "Yes, sir, it was. By 2 hens. And the captured stores will be arriving shortly for your breakfast."

By Easter 1945, 2 Commando had been moved out of the line and back to a base near Ravenna, where they began a short training programme with an unusual emphasis on navigation and boating. Jos' list of things to pack for the new mission included, along with usual items like 'sterilizing outfits' and 'field and shell dressings', strange extras like 'rubber boots' and a 'Mae West' inflatable life-jacket. They were about to participate in an important amphibious attack, Operation Roast, part of the big new Allied offensive of Spring 1945.

The British 8th Army, held up from its push into the north Italian towns like Bologna and Ferrara by a heavily concreted German line protecting the Po valley, was about to mount a bold attempt to burst through the Argenta Gap, a well-defended area between Lake Commacchio and the Lombardy marshes. Operation Roast would secure the army's right flank, by capturing Porto Garibaldi and a coastal area immediately to its south, on the far side of Lake Commacchio, a strongly garrisoned 5-mile spit of land, 1-mile wide, with three canals cut through it, linking the Adriatic with Lake Comacchio. The several thousand Germans defending this coastal area were expecting an attack from the sea, so the Commandos decided to surprise them with an amphibious assault from the opposite direction, across Lake Comacchio, something the Germans had ruled out, since Commacchio, far from being a navigable lake, was a vast swamp with just a few inches of water above an oozy slime several feet deep.

In the battle plan, the various different areas of the spit were given names from the Bible. To the south of the spit: Hosea 1 and 2, Matthew, Leviticus and Joshua; in the centre: Isaiah 1 and 2, Acts, Peter and Amos; to the north, leading towards the final objective of Porto Garibaldi: James and Jeremiah. While simultaneous attacks would come in by land from two other commando units to the south, 2 Commando and 9 Commando were to cross the lake by night, 2 Commando landing half-way up the spit just to the north of one of the canals, with 9 Commando some distance to the south of them. 2 Commando were then to turn south to the land of Isaiah, so that the Nazis there would find themselves attacked from two directions. A drive northwards was to ensue, through James and Jeremiah, culminating in the capture of Porto Garibaldi.

Operation Roast began on the night of Easter Monday, 2 April, with a last meal for Jos's Troop ("meat and vegetable stew") in a field below the village of Mandriole. When it was sufficiently dark they moved off in single file to the river Reno and were ferried across the river. The Royal Army Service Corps had brought the boats as far as the river, but the commandos were thereafter on their own, their first task being to carry the boats one and a half miles through deep mud to the edge of the lake. Flat-bottomed, with solid wooden ribs covered with canvas, the boats (plus their outboard motors, oars and other equipment) each weighed well over a ton.

Then came our first journey into the mud. At first I trod gingerly, worried about getting water in through the top of my boots, but as time got shorter and the boat could only be inched along, I tried to forget about the battle that would have to be fought in the morning and splashed around madly in the quagmire. We were soon all up to our knees in the glutinous mud. Each crew and boat sought its own salvation. Troops and sections became inextricably intermingled. When we eventually arrived in the 'harbour' area, it was almost midnight and we were an hour behind schedule.

The dark mass of the lagoon was faintly visible, stretching away into a distant horizon obscured by the black night. There was no jetty against which to moor the boats, and it took another three hours before the various components of 2 Commando had found each other and, in total darkness, re-assembled into an organized formation. Ted Fynn anxiously rang his Brigadier to say they were now several hours behind schedule, but there was no possibility of postponement because the artillery bombardment of the coastal area had already begun. At around 3.00 in the morning, therefore, the six Troops started off on the crossing of Lake Comacchio.

By now the spit was being plastered by the massed guns of 56 Division –
150 guns in all – so the noise didn't matter . . . The crescendo of noise that
bellowed across the lake as more and more craft started up was only slightly
louder than the clatter of the pull-start cords being furiously jerked by
men operating the flywheel starters on reluctant engines, while the Troop
commanders circled the craft shouting advice.

The four boats of Jos's Troop were soon experiencing problems. Though
the engines were large and powerful, high speed proved impossible in the
shallow and treacherous waters. And it was not long before Jos's boat hit a
sandbank.

There was no telling where the sandbank began or where it ended. The
other three boats in our Troop circled nearby while our engine was switched
off. (There was no neutral gear.) Paddles were used to try to back away, and
when that was unsuccessful men jumped overboard to try to lighten the
load. Eventually she was floated clear . . .

Apart from the hidden sandbanks, navigation was fairly easy. There were
red pilot lights on kayaks moored at three key points, though the flash of
bursting shells on the skyline was a stronger indication that they were going
in the right direction. The maintaining of a decent speed, however, was
more difficult. As they passed the third light, halfway across the lake, Jos's
boat spluttered and stopped with a seized engine, forcing them to complete
the crossing by pushing and paddling with their oars. Phosphorous shells
were still pounding German positions and dawn was beginning to break as
Jos and his desperately weary men scrambled over the final mud and slush
to dry land, the fourth and last of the six Troops to make the appointed
rendez-vous. Colonel Ted Fynn was there to meet them. "We need you to
capture Amos as soon as possible."

To capture Amos they first had to take the railway bridge over the
Bellocchio Canal. There was no time for planning or reconnaissance.

Low-lying mist was restricting visibility to 20 yards. Our Troop fanned out
and started moving through saplings in the direction of the bridge. There in
front was an open space and a sand-mound behind it. A single shot rang out
from the mound. Our bren gunners who had moved to a flank opened up
on it. Just at that moment there was a terrific explosion. Exactly what I had
feared. The enemy had blown up the bridge. Eerily, behind the sand mound

a solid slab of concrete seemed to lift itself up and then drop out of sight. We rushed forward, but it was too late. The sides of the single-line bridge tipped crazily into the Canal . . .

With the land on the far side of the bridge now completely inaccessible, Jos led his Troop in the other direction, northwards. His account of the subsequent fighting in *The Cross Still Stands* is extremely terse: "We came under intense fire. Part of the rifle group got cut off and had to lie in a water-logged ditch three hours." In writing this, he modestly omits the first of two actions which were to win him the Military Cross. Fortunately the award's citation gives rather more information:

Nicholl led his Troop 800 yards across open country in broad daylight, under heavy small arms fire from uncharted weapon pits – personally destroying several of these and one Spandau post. Later in the day, he again led his Troop against a strongly defended gun position. Although his Troop suffered a number of casualties from small arms and gun fire at point-blank range, Nicholl infiltrated with a bren team and harassed the position with such tenacity that the enemy gunners were forced to withdraw.

By next morning the Royal Engineers had thrown up a rough replacement bridge over the canal, allowing other units to sweep up through Amos and link up with 2 Commando in the push northwards in the direction of Porto Garibaldi. With some Sappers clearing mines and a few Churchill tanks in support, Jos's group swept all before them. His own account (of German mortar fire and the commandos' attempts to "winkle out observation posts") again omits his personal involvement. The citation of his award, however, states:

During the advance up the split, his Troop was leading when it was pinned down by vicious mortar and small arms fire. Nicholl, with great coolness and disregard for his own safety, visited his forward sections and rallied his men for a further advance. He was awarded an immediate MC.

By nightfall the mission was virtually complete. The commandos controlled most of the area from Hosea 2 in the south to Jeremiah in the north. Porto Garibaldi had fallen.

There was some more desultory fighting the next morning, but the three-day action was over, and the threat to the 8th Army on its east flank totally nullified. The four commando units involved in the operation had knocked out three complete enemy battalions, taking well over 1,000 German prisoners. 2 posthumous VCs were awarded.

On 8 April 1945, the day after the battle ended, Colonel Ted Fynn called a special parade for 2 Commando. After briefly outlining the remarkable results of the operation, he came to the major point of the gathering. "It has been," he said, "what amounts to little short of a miracle. And I believe that there was a Power behind it quite apart from any man-made agency." He thereupon asked the new Padre to lead their prayers of thanks to almighty God.

There was still one final challenge for 2 Commando: participating in a back-up role in the big attack (Operation Fry) now to be made through the Argenta Gap by the 8th Army. Shortly before going into action for the last time, Jos heard again from Olive. This time, in addition to the usual chocolates and biscuits, she had sent him a short poem.

Not merely in the words you say,
Not only in the deeds confessed,
But in the most unconscious way
Is Christ expressed.

And from your eyes He beckons me,
And from your heart His love is shed
Till I lose sight of you and see
The Christ instead.
      ('In-Dwelling', by A.S. Wilson)

The sentiments were as humbling and moving as the valedictory comments in the accompanying letter, but, for the moment at least, all Jos would have been able to do was to thrust it into a pocket as he and 2 Commando made their way to the small town of Conselice.

Their mission was to secure the 8th Army's extreme west flank, which would involve knocking out several Nazi blockhouses. This time (with Jos now leading 4 Troop in the hastily restructured unit), instead of attacking Biblical targets, they were advancing into a land of tobacco, the planners having given the operational area the names of cigarette manufacturers. A night advance from Conselice, therefore, led 2 Commando to Players, which they successfully assaulted on 16 April. Next day they met fierce resistance at Churchmans, and Jos and 4 Troop at one stage found themselves in a desperate position, pinned down by German fire:

It was a question of defending the rearward slope. For every movement over the ridge brought a hail of fire from the other side. Voices could be heard. The Germans were preparing an attack over the ridge.

Jos arranged his men as best he could to meet the expected charge.

But the first thing to arrive was a German stick grenade. It bounced against the side of the track and then fell into the water of the dyke below.

A battle of grenades ensued, Jos urging his men to hurl absolutely everything they had. The British Mills grenades found their mark more unerringly than the enemy's, and soon the Germans could be heard vacating their positions. But it was still time to be cautious:

Lying flat, we could just see them, to fire at. But one bright spark, thinking they would make an easy target, stood up and fired his rifle from the shoulder. There was a rapid burst from a machine-gun and the poor lad fell back, shot through the head . . .

There were still several days of fighting. On the 18th they attacked Abdullah, on the 19th Piccadilly and on the 20th made a cautious exploration of Black Cat, only to find, to their joy, that the Germans had retreated. The tide of the battle of Argenta Gap had turned, and Jos's war ended, somewhat bizarrely, in "doing a spot of town liberating":

On Saturday 21 April, across fields to my left, I could see the small town of Molinella. There were flags flying. Was this the last outpost of the German army? I decided to find out. As we approached the village, there was no doubt about it - the Germans had gone and the crowds were out to welcome the conquering heroes! I decided to make the most of it, giving orders for the men to fall out. They quickly disappeared into different houses to be fed with wine and omelettes. Then we made our way through the clapping throng to the piazza for an official welcome.

Finally, in a move which slightly smacked of an Alec Guinness Ealing comedy, Jos persuaded the villagers to provide him and his exhausted troop with a fleet of bicycles on which they could return to their base along the flat open country roads. Not only did the townsfolk swiftly produce them, but insisted on providing a grateful escort, riding alongside their liberators.

Only a week later a Nazi surrender document was being signed at General Alexander's headquarters in Caserta, and on 2 May 1945, when the Allies had been convinced that the document would be totally respected, the war in Italy was formally brought an end. Jos was in a makeshift mess at a makeshift base when he first heard about it:

Well, what tremendous news. 'All organized resistance in Italy has ceased.' I happened to be listening to the wireless at half-past-ten last night and got the news flash 'Herr Hitler is dead'. There were three of us there and we just looked up and then went on reading. And I suppose that is the event that poor schoolchildren will have to remember in days to come—that one who thought himself to be a God died on 30 April 1945. Funnily enough the others listening to the radio were Bob Bavister and Guy Whitfield, the only two officers left who came out with me from Blighty . . .

The news was hard to take in. So much had happened in the two continuous years Jos had been abroad with the commandos. So many friends had come and gone. He reflected gratefully to his parents:

I've always prayed to be given strength rather than safety, and in His Glorious Will He has provided me with both.

# 24

## DAVID AND JOANNA

Jos had long been aware of how fond David had become of his sister. In December 1944 he had told his parents:

Got a delightful letter from David . . . quite delightful. Dear David told me just what I had already read between the lines, and told it so delightfully, and was of course so absolutely charming about Joanna . . .

In mid-February 1945 when David was again visiting Ades on leave, Joanna greeted him with an airy "You know, I'm *not* going to marry you!" "I haven't asked you," he countered. But thereupon he did, and, to the great delight of both families, she at once accepted.

Jos had been fighting in the trenches north of Ravenna when news of the engagement came through. He immediately "gave three jumps for joy" and scribbled just one word in his diary: "Whoopee!" As soon as circumstances allowed, he wrote a letter to her full of superlatives. Such a union of the Nicholls and Carters, he declared, was like one of those denouements on stage when a Deus ex Machina suddenly takes over and imposes at one fell swoop the happiest of endings. It really was marvellous! To think it was David she was going to marry! "No-one needs to sing his praises in our ears because we all know him for what he is and love him for it . . ."

Although David's devotion to Joanna had been very obvious for the past two years, and no visits south from Scotland passed without his seeing her, Joanna was an independent young lady (at 20, eight years David's junior) and perhaps felt a little pressurised by the rest of the family's total devotion to David. As a trainee nurse, moreover, she had found herself the object of enough admiration from several personable young doctors to cause quite a few tremors of anxiety at Ades. Jos, from a distance, had been reassuring:

Mother darling, I'm not in the least bit worried about our Joanna. I know exactly how she feels. It's like trying all the different fruits in the garden before deciding that the one that one's been told is the best *is* the best . . .

And now at last his confidence had been vindicated!

Joanna later recalled that, at the time of the engagement, she and David shared together two verses from Exodus "which we reversed, for our needs", focusing first on the prayer: "If thy presence go not with me, carry us not up hence"; and then the reassuring answer: "My presence will go with thee, and I will give thee rest". These verses became very precious to them, "ones we always shared at the times our lives threatened to take on a new direction".

David, c.1946

Joanna, c.1944, the link between the two families

The wedding was fixed for late June, so, when the war in Europe suddenly ended, Jos's hopes of getting home in time rose a little. In May he was writing to his parents:

Delightful letter from Joanna giving details of W Day. (But, really, Joanna, you must be more careful with your choice! Don't you realize that there is a Victory Test Match on at Sheffield and a Varsity cricket match at Lord's the same day?) . . . The powers that be just can't decide what to do with us or else are purposely keeping us in the dark . . . But please don't give up all hope of my being able to attend the wedding.

He was still stranded near Ravenna, when his award of the Military Cross was officially announced. Among the letters which reached him there was one from Colonel Ted Fynn, who was already back in England. ("Many congratulations . . . I suppose you've had more Bosche ironmongery of various shapes and sizes thrown at you than anyone else in the Group. Good show, Joe.") His parents' comment that the award was "long deserved" elicited a cautionary response on the subject of his own "intolerable pride":

I had to learn the lesson of humility. It came as such a shock to me to find I had taken the gong so much for granted. I had even imagined that I had deserved it. But now I know that the glory should never have been mine – Not I but Christ – and that I should have been humbled to realize that the one who plants and the one who waters are nothing but Christ who gives the increase . . . .

David, still working as hard as ever with the Trials Unit, was similarly detached from the prevailing bullish atmosphere, as he prepared for the summer wedding, and took time out to write Joanna the most loving of letters, only to be opened if he should be killed, in which he urged her not to hesitate from marriage if the right man were to come along "and you know you are one in the Saviour's Love". They would meet again, he told her, in such glorious fellowship that even the wonderful union of marriage would seem a restrictive and imperfect one.

Fortunately his fears of a flying accident proved groundless, and they were duly married on 23 June 1945 at the village church of Chailey, just three days after Joanna's 21st birthday. David's eldest brother, the Revd. Roderick Carter, who had recently taken over a parish at Woking, led much of the service, though he almost missed it, his venerable motorbike and sidecar having broken down en route. The sidecar, moreover, contained the organist. Joanna later recalled:

We planned a quiet wedding, but by the summer of 1945 peace had been declared and everyone wanted to celebrate it too! It was a time of shortages but Pop's patients were generous in gifts of food and presents. Petrol coupons were shared to allow the families to gather. Dress material was in short supply, but generous folk donated clothing coupons for wedding dress material and a petticoat was made from the silk of one of David's parachutes!

After the service, children from Joanna's Sunday School lined the paths and, for the first time since the War, the bells of St Michael's, Chailey, were fully rung.

David and Joanna on their wedding day, Chailey, 1945

Jos, in the event, only missed the wedding by the barest of margins. He had headed off from Naples on the first of a series of transport ships just three days beforehand, and reached Southampton just two days after it was all over, finally arriving at Ades on an extended leave only hours before Joanna and David returned from their week's honeymoon. He had not seen Joanna for two years or David for three. A week later, they met up again in a wan-looking London, where, amid the many awful bomb craters and damaged buildings, their shared joy was an expression of a determination to make the very most of better times ahead, won at such heavy cost. After visiting the Royal Academy, they lunched, for just this one special occasion, at the Trocadero.

# 25
# PEACETIME

David did not leave the Navy immediately, introducing Joanna to several Naval Air Stations in the first year of marriage. Initially they were in Scotland, as David completed his work with the Service Trials Unit, its conclusion being marked with an MBE in the New Year's Honours List of 1946 ("for distinguished service during the war in Europe"). Afterwards, David worked for a time in the south of England as a Flying Instructor, commanding 799B Squadron at Gosport and Lee-on-Solent.

They were exciting times. On one occasion the bull-nosed Morris 'Archie' developed a puncture as they were crossing Salisbury Plain late at night. As David had forgotten that his spare tyre was punctured, he and Joanna found themselves stranded in the open little tourer, as cold winds swept over the pitch-dark countryside. Joanna long remembered the lengthy walk which followed.

I was beginning to learn about David's dear absent-mindedness, and his desire to extend the possible into the impossible. But his calmness in all situations never ceased to amaze me . . . !

At Lee-on-Solent David spent much of the time sleeping by day and flying by night, and soon had invented an original system of letting Joanna know when he'd be home, so that a hot drink could be ready.

The Harvard used to make a loud, distinctive noise, when flown in a certain way, so a friend of his would fly over our house, making this roaring noise, to alert me to his arrival.

Having recently learnt to glide, David would sometimes playfully swoop over their bungalow, which was not always to Joanna's total liking.

I didn't mind watching the normal gliding, but when he started to loop the loop I had to rush indoors!

In the autumn of 1946 David was persuaded by the Headmaster of his old school, St Lawrence, Ramsgate, to return as a Housemaster. One of his colleagues there, Bob Drayson (later Headmaster of Stowe), recalled:

He was a dear, dear man; one of the world's good men. As such, he might well have been found at one end of a St Lawrence classroom, sorting out a mathematical problem with one of the less gifted pupils, and quite oblivious of the goings-on at the other end. He ran his House on love. I ran mine on authority. Who is to say who was right? I have a sneaking suspicion he was!

The three years at Ramsgate were very happy ones. Their family life blossomed - two daughters, Heather and Rachel, were born in this period - and David thrived in his pastoral role. When he found boys difficult, recalled Joanna, he would often send them round to dig their garden.

After they'd done some work I'd give them some tea and cake, and very often the whole of their problems would come pouring out . . .

Jos, for his part, was also interested in teaching, and a quotation from *Henry V* (once a set book at school) about the aftermath of war had stayed with him throughout his commando days:

. . . And in him that escapes, it were not sin to think that, making God so free an offer, he let him outlive that day to see his greatness, and to teach others how they should prepare . . .

Unlike David, however, Jos first needed to acquire some further qualifications and so, in the autumn of 1945, he returned to Cambridge to finish his history degree (and play rugby for the university) before embarking on theological studies at Ridley Hall.

Not long before this return to Queens' College, Jos went down to Bude to help for a few days at a children's mission holiday.

Jos and Hope on their engagement

It was 15 August 1945, VJ Day (Victory in Japan). Shortly before catching the train, he had heard the new Prime Minister, Clement Attlee, tell the nation of the end of hostilities in the East, and an evening broadcast by King George VI was now eagerly awaited. Having arrived at Bude early, Jos took the opportunity to revisit some favourite haunts with a walk along the top of the cliffs. Finding a sheltered spot looking out to sea, he sat down, his mind full of Atlee's speech, oblivious of the bench's other occupant. A familiar voice broke through the reverie. He looked up. It was Hope Parry, who was also working as a volunteer at the very same summer camp! They had remained largely out of touch since Jos's proposal three years earlier, but it proved an auspicious reunion, and although Jos was no nearer to earning his living than he had been in 1942 and his decision to go into the church would mean further studies after the completion of his degree, the romance found swift renewal and this time had a happy ending. Not many months later Jos and Hope were engaged, and in June 1947, while Jos was still studying at Ridley Hall, they were married.

Jos speaking at a CSSM camp, Bude, 1946

The ceremony took place in Hope's home church in Surrey (Sanderstead) but Jos's close ties with All Souls Church, Langham Place, led to its Rector, Harold Earnshaw-Smith, officiating, along with his young curate, John Stott, who sang 'My Song Is Love Unknown' during the signing of the register.

Ordained in 1948, Jos himself was soon an enthusiastic young curate, working at Penge in Surrey (where his first two children, Angela and Tony, were born). In 1950 he finally responded to that exhortation from Henry V and went into teaching, becoming chaplain at Sutton Valence School, where, in addition, he ran a junior boarding house. He was also playing top-class rugby for London Irish, renewing his links with 'Bash' Nash's camps at Iwerne Minster and delighting in a busy family life, recently made all the busier by the arrival of two more children, Richard and Jonathan.

In 1959 he moved (as he had always hoped he might) to his old school, Stowe, where he was to spend the major part of his working life. The much-admired founder-headmaster J.F. Roxburgh was no longer alive, but the eighteenth-century campus was still a joy, particularly to a historian, and it was a lovely place in which to bring up a young family. Richard later recalled his happy childhood:

As a father, he instilled in his children a remarkable sense of assurance and well-being; an unquestioning confidence that he could be trusted completely, which one only came to appreciate with adulthood in seeing that that's not how all the world goes; as children we took it for granted, and it was the most fantastic basis for developing a trust in an entirely reliable Heavenly Father – because we had had it modelled for us."

The peace of the Stowe landscape gardens, with their crumbling temples and romantically overgrown vistas, was as far removed from the scorched battlefields of Italy as could be, yet Jos was never to forget them. Richard's elder brother, Tony, recalls that "Hardly a sermon went by without a war-time tale to teach us something of faith, courage, persistence and God's hand guiding and leading . . ."

By the time Jos arrived at Stowe, David, by contrast, had moved on from teaching. "With his pioneering spirit," remembered Joanna, "and his determination to help the less fortunate in life, he constantly needed fresh pastures" and this led in 1950 to the founding of a boys' probation home. David's parents had just decided to move out of High Beech, which was now far too big for them, so David, seizing his moment, persuaded the London Police Court Mission to acquire it, build on an extra wing, and open it as a forward-looking short-stay home, underpinned by its Christian commitment and a strong educational programme, with himself as the first Warden. Within a couple of years High Beech was looking after nearly fifty boys, all of whom had been in trouble with the law, and many regular offenders. Here David's natural patience was tested to the full. "There were many very dangerous young men at High Beech," recalled his matron, "but by showing respect and courtesy to them all David somehow managed to elicit those qualities from them." Good, of course, did not miraculously prevail all the time over evil. It was a constant struggle. The boys were for ever getting into trouble. On the very day High Beech opened, as parents and governors were relaxing on the lawn, some of the first residents were quietly removing lead from the roof. It was a tough challenge. "It has only been when we have allowed the Holy Spirit to guide this work," David wrote to his committee after the first year, "that we have made any progress." But the caring family atmosphere worked and progress was very real. Altogether 1,600 young delinquents were to experience the unique opportunities which High Beech offered before it finally closed in the late 1970's.

High Beech, where David founded a Probation Home for the
London Police Court Mission

David and Joanna, however, moved on after five years, the arrival of their third child, Robert, precipitating David's decision to join Hawker Siddeley, first as a test pilot and later as a development adviser (development including the supersonic Hawker Hunter which, by the mid-50s, was breaking world speed records). It was a wonderful job, involving interesting travel. But having been deeply shocked on a business trip to India by all the poverty and squalor he saw there, he felt constrained to try to do something about it. One image, in particular, haunted him: the view, from the air, of mile after mile of wasted, infertile land. And so he transferred to Armstrong Whitworth to work on a new idea: a Land Development Aircraft which would answer the agricultural needs of underdeveloped countries. He eventually founded his own company ("Mannair–to feed the world") and attempted to persuade the chemical manufacturers and aircraft constructors to back "an aircraft to help free the world from hunger", specifically designed to combat large areas of barren waste. Such a project, his promotional booklet explained, would altruistically "put people before profits". But in the event, despite much travel and many meetings, he eventually had to face up to the sad fact that, for the world, profits still came before people.

Joanna and David in the late 1950s with Heather, Rachel and Robert, Hayward's Heath

If he couldn't help the undeveloped countries, he could at least try to help others closer to home. Turning back to education, he acquired a lovely old house in the heart of the Sussex downs, Northease Manor, just outside Lewes, and turned it into a small secondary school for boys who had hitherto struggled with their work.

A family gathering of Nicholls and Carters at Castle Lodge,
Lewes, in the early 1960s with David and Jos in the back row
and Hope and Joanna among those seated

David, Joanna, Hope and Jos at Northease Manor, mid-1960s

At the time there was little in the way of remedial teaching. Dyslexia had
not yet been generally recognised as a problem. But David had researched
it and had big ambitions for his pupils. "This is a school," he wrote in
his first prospectus, "for boys whose characters are likely to benefit their

fellow men." He eliminated any mention of past failure and concentrated on the idea of service to others: "The school stands uncompromisingly on Christian foundations and aims at developing complete men capable of moral leadership in the outside world."

Northease Manor School, Sussex, founded by David and Joanna

David's notebooks were full of thoughts jotted down as he prepared for this new venture. One Sunday in 1962, very early on in the planning stage, taking as his text Isaiah's 'Thou art my servant; I have chosen thee and not cast thee away', he wrote:

When you meet difficult people, remember
(a) They are God's children and He wants them for Himself.
(b) To pray and pray and PRAY for them
(c) To pray and pray and PRAY for wisdom to understand them and HELP them.
All that has gone before - the difficult people and situations - has been a training ground for the task ahead.

Shortly before he opened the school, with just 6 pupils in 1963, he wrote in his diary:

The house to be a house of Miracles for young and old. A house where people begin to be more like God intended them to be. A place where everyone LIVES LIFE TO THE FULL. Where care for each individual, however few we have, means that he can start to grow in grace and favour ... We have been entrusted with a message. The delivery of this message is to be in God's time and way. The secret you have - available every moment - is that IN THE NAME OF JESUS CHRIST lies the POWER by which all God's purpose can be fulfilled; that it is HE ALONE who changes the direction of young or old and develops God-like character; that it is your part to be obedient.

The project proved a huge success in every way. Numbers rose steadily to the absolute maximum of 50, coped for by further building works and development. Successful inspections led to early Ministry of Education recognition. And, for all the many problems along the way, Northease really did become a 'House of Miracles'.

David had gained much inner strength from that defining moment in his life when he was flying in the clouds between the Scottish mountainsides in his Albacore. One early-morning entry in his Northease diary movingly employs imagery from that occasion:

For you, the setting of your gyro direction indicator means the decision to abide by and commit your life absolutely to the directional standards of God, without fear of the hazards of this new course and totally without regard to past ups and downs ... God's directional course depends upon four compass-points which emerge clearly from the teaching of Jesus: absolute standards of honesty, purity, unselfishness and love. "Let go! Set your gyro! Fly straight! Now climb!"

The long hours and emotional intensity of the job gradually took their toll. But it was as exhilarating as it was tiring. Less than a year before he died, for example, he was writing in his diary:

Tiredness? I suppose I was dead tired yesterday. But it was such a wonderful day of healing!

Despite all the pressures and problems, David contrived to remain rejoicing and optimistic. His zest for life shines through his last notebook, as does his love for his family. On the morning of his last birthday, he wrote, "I feel so grateful for Joanna, Heather, Rachel and Robert", and on the occasion of his silver wedding, four months before he died:

It was Joanna's selflessness that captured me in the first place and has held me ever since. And then it was her ability to say sorry and mean it. I thank her so deeply for that. Her response to the best: 'It's not what I want or what you want that matters. It's what God wants.'

David died at Northease very suddenly, at only 54, after coming back to the house after a game of hockey. That very morning, on 26 October 1970, he had written in his notebook:

Thinking about a film the school saw on Saturday evening, the verse came to me: 'Do not fear those who kill the body but cannot kill the soul.'

To this he had added:

'Death is swallowed up in victory. Oh death, where is thy sting?'

David at Northease shortly before his death

The tragic suddenness of David's death came as a most terrible shock for everyone who loved and knew him. But Joanna and the family bravely kept the school going and, in due course, it became a state-funded boarding school, which has allowed further, sympathetic development of the lovely site. Its 50<sup>th</sup> anniversary is now not far away.

In their different ways both David's and Jos's post-war lives were fuelled by a determination to counter the forces of evil they had so vividly witnessed in the war to the best of their abilities. And the words which Jos wrote in 1945 for a small book of Christians' wartime experiences, were to be exemplified by the way David met the different challenges he imposed upon himself:

Jesus Christ provides the inspiration for every possible occasion or need. He can act as guide and helper and comforter, but primarily He can be the driving force in a life that is devoted to Him, and with this compelling power behind them it becomes true in practice that 'the people that do know their God shall be strong and do exploits'.
(*Experience Will Decide*)

David and Joanna had kept in close touch with Jos and Hope throughout the past twenty-five years. In the 1960s, indeed, they had shared a common interest in Stowe, for, at the time of David's death, his son Robert was just completing his sixth-form career there. And Robert was in the same Stowe boarding house as Jos's sons Richard and Jonathan. It was natural, therefore, that Jos helped at David's Memorial Service at Southover Church, Lewes, and, in the course of it, read the moving conclusion from John Bunyan's *The Pilgrim's Progress* (a book he had taken with him on his commando travels).

Jos, at fifty, was now well-established at Stowe, one of the big characters on the staff there, a much respected Housemaster, Chaplain and teacher of history. His sermons and talks were distinctly less fiery than in the wartime. In the school chapel, indeed, in order to gain the attention of a congregation who were mostly not present from choice, he would regularly resort to biblical language, though this was usually studded arrestingly with allusions to contemporary figures and events. (One such diversion, shortly after a record football transfer, began: "And verily, one day, there came forth a young man, Trevor Francis from the Forest of Nottingham . . . ."). His wartime experiences often made for fascinating diversions. His daughter Angela remembers a typical example - during a sermon on the Faith of the Centurion ("I tell this one, 'Go' and he goes; and that one, 'Come' and he comes") – when Jos suddenly brought in President Tito, whose name, in his own language, meant 'come and go'.

Jos and Hope at Cobham House, Stowe, with (l.-r.) son-in-law Peter, daughter Angela, grandson Tim, and sons Richard, Jonathan and Anthony

In 1975, at the age of 55, Jos gave up his Boarding House and combined his history teaching with being Vicar of Stowe Church. Tucked away in the school's grounds, surrounded by trees, this pretty little church serves a village which Stowe's eighteenth-century creator (the not very godly Lord Cobham) had swept aside and repositioned two miles away, as he created his new landscape gardens. Over two hundred years later, the villagers were still making the two-mile journey to the church. Jos wrote contentedly in a welcoming booklet:

We are a tiny parish as far as numbers go, but on Sundays a worshipping congregation uses this Church. Sometimes we are not many; sometimes the Church is full. But we come "to offer our Lord Jesus Christ our worship and praise and thanksgiving; to make confession of our sins; to pray for others as well as ourselves, that we may know more truly the greatness of God's love, and shew forth in our lives the fruits of His Grace".

Padre Gareth Banting would have hugely approved.

Jos and Hope flanked by friends outside Stowe Church, mid-1970s

The commando in Jos still emerged each Wednesday afternoon, when, immaculate in khaki and green beret, he devised for the Army section of the Combined Cadet Force ever more challenging assault courses in the woods and dropped the odd unexpected thunderflash behind the laggardly and lordly, bringing a touch of Achnacarry to the sleepy Buckinghamshire countryside. (With one of his thunderflashes, so legend has it, he inadvertently sank a small craft being used on a Stowe lake in a CCF inter-house competition.)

Jos retired from Stowe in 1982, but still had much to offer: as Rector of Angmering for 3 years; as chaplain to St Peter's, Chantilly; at the English churches in Lyons and Grenoble at Christmas times. Having settled with Hope in his beloved Lewes, he became a valued assistant at Malling Church as well as chairman of the Bible Society Action Group and the Lewes Council of Churches. When *Songs of Praise* visited the county town for Bonfire Night, Jos led the outdoor service.

Jos in the early 1980s, a long-serving officer in the Stowe School cadet force

He was also, chaplain to Royal Air Force Association, the British Legion and the Commando Association, assisting his Cambridge contemporary, Bishop Maurice Wood, at many of the services at the Commando Memorial near Achnacarry. He never forgot his commando comrades, regularly attending reunions and on several occasions revisiting distant battlefields. He spoke the eulogy at Colonel Jack Churchill's funeral in 1997.

Hope was his ever-present companion, confidante, helper and partner in Christ. As she herself commented (in one of the many talks she gave), "All the way through, as long as we put God first and trusted Him for strength, He has never failed." When she died in 2001, Tim LeRoy, the eldest of Jos and Hope's ten much-loved grandchildren, delightfully summed up the homely and orderly household which Hope for over fifty years had so devotedly provided:

Jos and Hope with their family on their Ruby Wedding

Granny's heaven will be a place of warm Ribena, drunk through spoon straws on a Sunday morning. It will have the breakfast table laid out the night before, with a fine net cloth laid over to protect the crockery from Aga soot. There will be Corgis and crochet and soft cardigans. There will be bird-tables and hanging nut-baskets and all the chaffinches and blue-tits will crowd around the window to be noted and appreciated . . .

Already frail, Jos was very lost after Hope's death, despite the comfort of a large and loving family. Just as in the immediate aftermath of the war, when he had suffered recurring nightmares of the atrocities he had witnessed, so, too, in his final days of frailty, some of the wartime horrors became once more a vivid reality to him. He died in a Frome nursing home aged 83, in July 2003, eighteen months after Hope.

At a service of thanksgiving for his life, held at Stowe Church, his son Richard recalled:

Dad's last years were hard for him and sad to witness, and it made us aware just how much Mum must have done to support him; but the same lovely, courteous man shone through. Even if yesterday was a complete haze, lines from Keats or amusing puns still tripped off his tongue, and memories from fifty years back were vivid. At Christmas he joined us for a family lunch at

Angela's; who was who was anyone's guess, but when invited to say Grace, we were treated to the most wonderfully clear and heartfelt thanksgiving. God was still strengthening and holding his spirit. And on his last morning, as he struggled for breath, I read to him those familiar verses from Romans 8, and his lips moved to form the words he knew so well: 'Nothing can separate us from the love of God in Christ Jesus our Lord.' We prayed with him and he mouthed a silent 'thank you' – ever courteous and appreciative . . .

The little church he knew and had served so well was full to overflowing on this occasion, the link with David all the stronger for the presence of Joanna, now in a wheelchair. In the course of the service, one of the grandchildren read extracts from Jos's wartime memoir, *The Cross Still Stands*.

Joanna herself died four years later, in January 2007 at the age of 82. Joanna's extrovert nature (which had made her a highly successful Mayor of Lewes, JP and prison visitor) had been a crucial help to David in his highly individual adventures, his talents and ideals being very much underpinned by her social skills and greater practicality. Joanna believed practising Christians should be buoyant people, having fun, and her strong faith never inhibited her contagious exuberance.

The concluding words from Bunyan's *The Pilgrim's Progress* were heard again at Joanna's funeral service, thirty-six years after Jos had read them in the service for David. For David and Joanna, Jos and Hope, no reading could surely have been more fittingly chosen:

'Then,' said Mr Valiant-for-Truth, 'I am going to my Father's; and though with great difficulty am I got hither, yet now I do not repent me of all the trouble I have been at to arrive where I am. My sword I give to him that shall succeed me in my pilgrimage, and my courage and skill to him that can get it. My marks and scars I carry with me, to be a witness for me, that I have fought his battles who will now be my rewarder.' When the day that he must go hence was come, many accompanied him to the river side, into which as he went he said, 'Death, where is thy sting?' And as he went down deeper, he said, 'Grave, where is thy victory?' So he passed over, and all the trumpets sounded for him on the other side.

# BIBLIOGRAPHY

Blissett, Capt. H.H.: *Salerno Diary*, Army Bureau of Current Affairs (private circulation only), March 1944

Churchill, Major-General T., *Commando Crusade*, William Kimber, London, 1987

Churchill, Winston, *The Second World War*, Cassell, 1964

Croft-Cooke, Rupert, *The Blood-Red Island*, Staples Press, London, 1953

Deakin, F.W.D., *The Embattled Mountain*, Oxford University Press, London, 1971

Eddison, John (Ed.), *BASH, A Study in Spiritual Power*, Marshalls, Basingstoke 1983

Hickey, Des & Smith, Gus: *Operation Avalanche*, Heinemann, London, 1983

Jameson, William, *Ark Royal 1939-1941*, Rupert Hart-Davis, London, 1957

Ladd, James, *Commandos & Rangers of World War II*, Macdonald & Jane's, London, 1978

Matthias, Edwin, *Chailey Through the Centuries*, privately published, 1996

Messenger, Charles, *The Commandos*, William Kimber, London, 1985

Neillands, Robin, *The Raiders*, Weidenfeld & Nicolson, London, 1989

Nicholl, J.E.C., *The Cross Still Stands*, unpublished ms

Nicholl, J.E.C. et alii, *Experience Will Decide*, Officers' Christian Union, London c.1945

Parker, John, *Commandos*, Headline, London, 2000

J.C. Pollock, *A Cambridge Movement*, John Murray, London, 1953

Preston, Antony, *Aircraft Carriers*, Hamlyn, Feltham, 1979

Rossiter, Mike, *Ark Royal*, Bantam Press, London, 2006

Tomlinson, Michael, *The Most Dangerous Moment*, William Kimber, London, 1976

Wragg, David, *The Fleet Air Arm Handbook, 1939-1945*, Sutton, Stroud, 2001

DAVID CARTER'S PRAYER AT CHRISTMAS
The conclusion of his Carol Service at Northease,
December 1969


Heavenly Father, make each moment of our lives a miracle. Make us laugh at the impossible. Give us hope when all things seem hopeless; peace, where no peace could be; love for the unlovable. Make us gamble all on your almightiness, and to dare everything in your great service.

Lightning Source UK Ltd.
Milton Keynes UK
UKOW050021241211

184360UK00001B/87/P